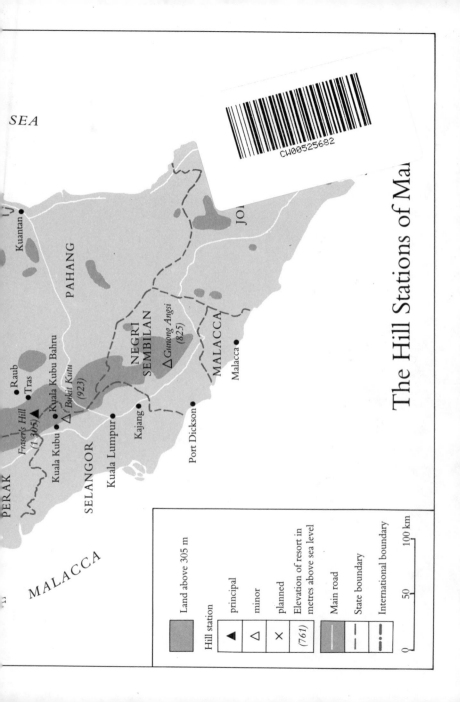

The Hill Stations of Mal

SEA

Kuantan

PAHANG

PERAK

Raub
Tras
Kuala Kubu Bahru
Fraser's Hill
(1,305)
Kuala Kubu
Bukit Kutu
(923)

NEGRI
SEMBILAN
△*Gunong Angsi*
(825)

MALACCA
Malacca

SELANGOR

Kuala Lumpur
Kajang
Port Dickson

JO

MALACCA

Hill station	
Land above 305 m	
▲	principal
△	minor
×	planned
(761)	Elevation of resort in metres above sea level

Main road	
State boundary	
International boundary	

0   50   100 km

IMAGES OF ASIA

Imperial Belvederes

Titles in the series

Imperial Belvederes
The Hill Stations of Malaya

S. ROBERT AIKEN

KUALA LUMPUR
OXFORD UNIVERSITY PRESS
OXFORD SINGAPORE NEW YORK
1994

Oxford University Press

Oxford New York Toronto
Delhi Bombay Calcutta Madras Karachi
Kuala Lumpur Singapore Hong Kong Tokyo
Nairobi Dar es Salaam Cape Town
Melbourne Auckland Madrid

and associated companies in
Berlin Ibadan

Oxford is a trade mark of Oxford University Press

Published in the United States
by Oxford University Press, New York

British Library Cataloguing in Publication Data
Data available

Library of Congress Cataloging-in-Publication Data
Aiken, S. Robert (Samuel Robert), 1942–
Imperial belvederes: the hill stations of Malaya/S. Robert Aiken.
p. cm.—(Images of Asia)
Includes bibliographical references and index.
ISBN 967 65 3037 9
1. Malaya—Description and travel.
2. Summer resorts—Malaya.
I. Title. II. Series.
DS592.5.A37 1994
959.5'1—dc20
93-31390
CIP

Typeset by Indah Photosetting Centre Sdn. Bhd., Malaysia
Printed by Kim Hup Lee Printing Co. Pte. Ltd., Singapore
Published by Oxford University Press,
19–25, Jalan Kuchai Lama, 58200 Kuala Lumpur, Malaysia

For Jane Barr, with love

I will lift up mine eyes unto the hills, from whence cometh my help.

—Psalm 121: 1

Preface

HILL stations owed their origin, early development, and widespread distribution to colonialism. Sometimes called 'change-of-air stations' or 'sanatoria', they were specialized highland outposts of colonial settlement that initially served as health-and-recreation centres for civil servants, planters, miners, and other expatriate Europeans, or as strategic bases and cantonments. Generally small and isolated, always defiantly out of place, they were insular little worlds that symbolized European power and exclusiveness. They were places apart. A metaphor that comes to mind is that of a belvedere, a lofty place with a commanding view. Perched as they invariably were on the ridges and flanks of mountain ranges, the hill stations were the belvederes of empire. Simla, the summer capital of the Raj, was the British belvedere *par excellence*.

Malaya had four principal hill stations: Penang Hill, Maxwell's (sometimes Maxwell) Hill, Fraser's Hill, and Cameron Highlands (see Endpapers). Penang Hill, situated on the lovely island of Penang, was established by the English East India Company in the late eighteenth century, which would appear to make it the oldest hill station in the British empire. The other three hill stations were positioned on the flanks of the Malay Peninsula's rugged spinal column, the Main Range, and they were developed in the 1880s, 1920s, and mainly 1930s, respectively. All four hill stations lacked most of the institutions that characterized their Indian counterparts. Small and only modestly developed, each was essentially a collection of bungalows. Only extensive Cameron Highlands experienced any appreciable growth, and that came mainly from the development of commercial agriculture, not from its role as a place of health-and-recreation.

Bungalows were erected on Gunong Kledang in Perak, on Bukit Kutu in Selangor, and on Gunong Angsi in Negri Sembilan in the 1890s and early 1900s, but none of these diminutive outposts of empire attracted any further growth, and a pre-World War I proposal to develop a grand hill station on the south side of Gunong Tahan, in northern Pahang, Malaya's highest mountain peak, failed to materialize (see Endpapers).

This book describes the origins, development, functional composition, and landscape characteristics of Malaya's hill stations and attempts, through a liberal sprinkling of quotations, to reveal how visitors to the hill stations passed their time and what they thought or felt about the experience. More specifically, it looks at some selected aspects of hill-station land and life in the Orient (Chapter 1), explores the genesis and development of Penang Hill and examines its role as a place of refuge (Chapter 2), outlines the reasons behind the growing demand for additional hill stations (Chapter 3), describes the development of the mainland hill stations (Chapter 4), and elucidates two themes in greater depth, namely, bungalows and gardens (Chapter 5) and social life and leisure (Chapter 6). The story covers the period from the early nineteenth century to World War II, although brief references to recent developments are made in the Epilogue.

Regardless of the time period under discussion, the terms 'Malaya' and 'the Peninsula' have been used interchangeably to describe the region extending from Singapore to the Thai border, although, strictly speaking, there was no such entity as 'Malaya' during the nineteenth century (see Chapter 3). The spelling of Malaysian toponyms poses certain problems because in recent times a good many familiar names have been replaced by new romanized Malay spellings: for example, Melaka instead of Malacca, Pinang rather than Penang, Gunung, not Gunong. Since this essay focuses entirely on the colonial period, I have opted for the older versions of the names.

I would like to thank Mildred Archer, Ray Desmond, Anthony D. King, Khoo Boo Chia, Colin H. Leigh, Datuk Lim Chong Keat, K. G. Tregonning, and Mary Turnbull for helping me with various queries over the years. My thanks go to the Oxford University Press for assistance with the illustrations and to Ms Tina Skalkogiannis for her careful typing of and other help with the manuscript. In particular, I gratefully acknowledge the good counsel of Dr John Bastin, formerly of the School of Oriental and African Studies, University of London, who kindly read and commented on a draft of the text.

Finally, I should point out that parts of this work draw on my essay in the 1987 volume of the *Geographical Review*.

Montreal   S. ROBERT AIKEN
January 1993

Contents

1
The Hill Station

HILL stations originated in the Netherlands East Indies and British India in the early nineteenth century, and this novel type of settlement soon appeared in other parts of Asia that came under colonial domination: for example, in British-ruled Burma, Ceylon (Sri Lanka), and Malaya; in Dutch-ruled Java, the Celebes (Sulawesi), and Sumatra; in French Indo-China; in the Philippines under American rule; and in China and Japan, where the hill-station idea was implemented by Occidental missionaries.

The colonial hill stations were very unevenly distributed. They were numerous in parts of India and Java, the innovative core areas of the old British and Dutch empires in the Orient, but elsewhere they were thinly scattered or absent altogether. In a seminal paper on the hill stations of tropical Asia, the geographers J. E. Spencer and W. L. Thomas related the pattern of distribution to the following factors: the total number of Europeans and the duration of their involvement in particular areas; the relative 'severity', as they put it, of the tropical climate; the nearness and accessibility of suitable highland sites; and the kinds of political relations that existed between Europeans and Asians. It is notable that a hill-station tradition did not develop in countries or regions that were not brought under direct European control: for example, Thailand and the Unfederated Malay States (UMS).

The purpose-built highland settlements were made possible by the ability of Europeans to command strategically important uplands, to build roads and railways into previously inaccessible hills and mountains, and to control and exploit the economies, natural resources, and peoples of subjugated lands. Accompanying these forces were certain attitudes towards peoples, places, and environments, certain socially and culturally prescribed behavioural patterns, and certain ways of looking at, building in, and shaping the landscape. As Anthony King shows in his *Colonial*

Urban Development, it was the socio-cultural background and experiences of the Europeans that provided the main rationale for the development of the hill stations.

But what, more exactly, was it that motivated Europeans to fashion a new form of colonial urban development in some of the most remote and isolated parts of the tropics? Just what did these little places mean? What kinds of ideas, attitudes, and values did they reflect and embody? An attempt is made here to answer these questions by looking at the hill stations as places of refuge and places of resort.

The hill stations were places of refuge from the perceived health hazards of the lowlands, which for the most part were thought to result from the baleful and pestiferous effects of the tropical climate. The inevitable result of a lengthy residence in the tropics, most Europeans believed, was a loss of mental and physical capacities. Since permanent residence in the low latitudes was out of the question, and since even temporary residence was, at best, perceived to be enervating and debilitating, most colonists felt that it was essential to return to a cool or temperate region periodically, there to recover strength and vitality prior to another tour of duty. In short, one rationale for the development of hill stations was that they obviated the necessity of a long and costly journey home by providing more accessible places with a benign, home-like climate that promised physical and emotional renewal.

Sickly white troops and civilians trekked to the hill stations in search of relief from malaria, dysentry, and other tropical maladies, and among the earliest structures in the highlands were convalescent bungalows. Only later, it would seem, did the upland outposts take on the additional role of preserving health, and it was not until the late nineteenth century that the British began to view certain of the Indian hill stations as suitably healthy places for retirement.

The hill stations were also, indeed primarily, resorts, that is to say, they were specialized social places that Europeans frequented for fun and relaxation, for social intercourse with family and friends, or for mere dalliance. The model for the British hill stations as places of resort was the metropolitan spa and the generally later seaside resort. This requires a brief explanation.

One sign of growing affluence in eighteenth-century England, according to the British historian J. H. Plumb, was the rise of socially emulative spending on holidays, music, drama, sports, and other leisure-time pursuits, all of which became increasingly commercialized. Accompanying this trend was the emergence and growth of specialized urban places that catered mainly to sojourners in search of leisure and amusement as well as votaries of health and rest. These new or invigorated urban places were spas and seaside resorts. Health benefits were believed to derive from taking the waters and from sea air and bathing, but the resorts became primarily social and recreational places. Consequently, they had assembly rooms for dances and music, race courses, theatres, and libraries, while other features like promenades and piers promoted alfresco social interaction. For a 'particular social class in the metropolitan society', as King observes (in the work already mentioned), 'a model of "dual residence" emerged comprising a permanent, usually winter, residence in the town and a temporary location, ostensibly for health but in reality equally for social-recreational reasons, in a "resort"'. It was the metropolitan resort that provided the point of reference for the hill station, which in turn, as King goes on to explain, 'provided in its physical, social, psychological and "aesthetic" climate, the closest approximation to conditions of life "at home".'

Detached from the alien land and life of the lowlands, secluded in the cool and airy highlands, built from scratch as separate, aloof little worlds, the hill stations offered exclusive milieux where sojourners could feel at home. Home was the model or ideal, for more than anything else the hill stations were replacement or substitute places—places that were intended to resemble and feel like well-loved distant homelands. No wonder that visitors to the highland resorts commented so frequently on their familiar-appearing landscapes and architecture, on their bracing air, their flowers and fruits from temperate climates, their neat little gardens, and on simple reminders of home like a fire in the hearth, a blanket on the bed. Nostalgia was the common experience of most visitors.

Apart from those with permanent military garrisons or sizeable indigenous communities, most hill stations catered primarily to temporary residents, the majority of whom were drawn from the principal towns and cities of the plains—from places like Bombay, Calcutta, Madras, Colombo, Rangoon, Kuala Lumpur, Singapore, and Batavia (Jakarta), all of which, by the way, were mainly European creations. Usually each of these places had its own hill station, sometimes more than one, with the result that regular patterns of movement were established between lowlands and highlands—between, for example, Bombay and Poona or Mahableshwar, Calcutta and Simla or Darjeeling, Mandalay and Maymyo, Kuala Lumpur and Fraser's Hill. In India, Burma, and other parts of Asia with a pronounced seasonal climate, sojourners took off for the hills during the hot and oppressive summer months, whereas in equatorial regions like Malaya, the seasonal cycle of movement was less distinct.

Reaching the hill stations required considerable determination because it was only after the motor car appeared on the scene that the journey became relatively easy. Prior to that time most travellers were confronted by the prospect of a slow, tedious, and laborious trek over sinuous, unpaved tracks or paths that clung to precipitous slopes, plunged into ravines, and zigzagged interminably upwards. Much depended on the traveller's state of health, age, and sex because these factors usually determined the chosen mode of transportation. Able-bodied males sometimes walked up but usually they made the ascent on a stout little hill-pony. Invalids and children were more likely to be carried in some kind of litter, perhaps in a doolie, a covered box-like contraption in which there was barely room to sit up, or perhaps in a palanquin, a covered litter carried by several bearers, which was usually furnished with shelves, an oil lamp, and a mosquito net. Most women also chose to be conveyed by bearers. In a book on Simla, Pat Barr observes that the jampan figured as an important mode of travel during the nineteenth century. This, she wrote, was 'a sort of sedan chair, fitted with curtains, strung on poles and carried by at least four bearers called jampanees'. Emily Eden, sister of Governor-General Lord Auckland, called these cramped conveyances 'upright coffins'. Where the ascent was somewhat easier, travellers and their various accoutrements were transported in bullock carts. In her book on Ootacamund (popularly called Ooty since the 1840s), the principal hill station of the Madras presidency, Mollie Panter-Downes writes that '[i]f you were young and vigorous, you rode. If you were older, or young and lazy, you could go by bullock cart or be carried in a palanquin.' It was not unusual for travellers to make the journey in stages, relying on different modes of conveyance, with stops along the way for rest and refreshment at dak bungalows or rest-houses.

A few of the better known hill stations were eventually linked to the lowlands by rail, thereby greatly enhancing their accessibility and popularity. In 1872, a narrow-gauge cog railway was constructed between Silgiri and Darjeeling, and it was along this line that a little toy train took travellers up through the forests and the tea plantations to the diminutive hill station, there to get a glimpse, if the weather was right, of numinous Kanchenjunga, or of Everest from nearby Tiger Hill. Something of the inexorable might of the Raj was reflected in the opening, in 1903, of the 96 kilometres of track between Kalka and Simla, an engineering feat that required numerous hair-raising reverse curves and more than one hundred tunnels—all this to reach 'the home of the heaven-born', 'the abode of the little tin gods' (Colour Plate 1). A good deal more modest was Penang Hill's funicular railway, which was eventually finished, after an abortive earlier attempt, in 1923. But generally speaking it was not until the inter-war years, when metalled roads were extended from the main towns and the motor car came into its own, that the hill stations became more accessible.

Most hill stations were small places, and some were diminutive. Two of a number of exceptions to the small-size rule were Baguio, the summer capital of the Philippines under American rule, and Buitenzorg (Bogor) on Java, the permanent seat of the Dutch executive in the Netherlands East Indies. Both were cities. Some hill stations occupied relatively flat or undulating plateaux, but most were confined to awkward, irregular sites with very little flat land. The result, in most cases, was that buildings were strung out along narrow ridges, perched on crags, bluffs, and eminences, and plastered in layers to the flanks of precipitous hillsides. The highest and most salubrious sites were occupied by the bungalows and villas of senior government officials, by good hotels, and by the private retreats of the well-to-do. Contour roads and connecting paths and stairways linked the layers of buildings along the slopes, descending until, at or near the bottom, they petered out in the jumbled bazaar and native quarters. There could be no mistaking the fact that elevation and social class were in tandem.

A prominent feature of the more important hill stations was a main street, mall, or esplanade. It was here that the more select shops were located, and it was here too that the visitor would probably find a library, a theatre, assembly rooms, a post office, a bandstand, vantage points from which to admire the view, and, perhaps at one end of the thoroughfare, a church—Anglican, of course, if it were a British hill station. Elsewhere there were various facilities or amenities for outdoor sports and recreation: a cricket pitch, a polo field, a racecourse, public or botanic gardens, walks and drives, perhaps a golf course—all these were typical of the British hill stations. It was all rather reminiscent, albeit in a very different setting, of the metropolitan resorts, and like those resorts the scene before the visitor—the buildings, the shops, the various attractions—was largely the product of private investment.

Whether on the plains or in the hills, no other building or construction was nearly so redolent or symbolic of the imperial presence as the bungalow, the basic residential unit of the colonial community. Typically, the bungalow was a low, oblong, spacious, one-storey dwelling with a pyramidal roof, a veranda on at least one, often on all, sides, and a *porte-cochère*. Invariably, it was well away from its neighbours and set in an extensive walled, hedged, banked, or otherwise clearly demarcated compound that also included a garden, a gravel drive running down to a roadside gate, and, to the rear of the dwelling, a kitchen, servants' quarters, a well, and storage space for conveyances. Virtually all bungalows were built by amateur architects, most of whom were military engineers or employees of Public Works Departments (PWDs), and many were given names reminiscent of England, sometimes of Scotland, or of fondly remembered flowers, fruits, or trees.

Carefully demarcated, more or less self-contained, distant from indigenous communities, dedicated to the nuclear family—nothing more clearly symbolized European separateness from the alien land and life all around than the bungalow in its own compound.

Hill-station bungalows and other buildings reflected a wide variety of architectural styles. At Simla, 'the larger buildings ranged in style from railway Gothic of the most overpowering kind to publican's Tudor', writes Michael Edwardes in *Bound to Exile*. The influences behind the styles, according to Jan Morris's *Stones of Empire*, included the exuberances of Strawberry Hill Gothic, a penchant for the cottage *orné*, and a fondness for the chalet styles of the Swiss and German Alps. 'Add to this,' she continues, 'a contemporary taste for ornamental woodwork, elaborate it with ... porches and verandahs ... festoon everything with guttering and down-pipes, cap it with a marvellous variety of convoluted chimney-pots, essential to the tone of the thing as to the brisk mountain climate, wrap it all up in the familiar imperial bungalow, and you have the fundamentals of the hill-station style.'

Most visitors to the British hill stations sought amusement in popular pursuits such as alfresco sports, games, and shows of one kind or another: croquet, lawn tennis, cricket, polo matches, horse-racing—above all horse-racing—gymkhanas, dog- and horse-shows, riding, and hunting. Other favourite pastimes included reading, writing, and sketching on the veranda, indulging in the hobby of collecting things, gardening, and, of course, visiting that ubiquitous institution, the Club. Occasionally, there was a ball to attend. Often there was little to do, especially for the women and children, except to go on another walk. Here is an extract from Anthony Trollope's description of Nuwara Eliya, Ceylon's principal highland resort, which he wrote for the *Liverpool Mercury* in 1875: 'I found a regular little England, enjoying itself in its holiday. Cricket-matches were going on, and there were kinds of football. It was a race-meeting week, and the place was full of races.... The racing was generally at eleven or twelve, after breakfast; but early in the morning we turned out and hunted the elk.... After the races there was cricket.... Then came a morning dance in the public room till dinner, and in the evening a ball. . . . There seemed to be no rest, except on Sunday, when a good deal of sleep was done, both in and out of church.'

The lifestyle that Trollope described rested on a foundation of inequality. Notably absent from his charming little sketch of Europeans at play is any mention of the battalions of labourers whose work made so much leisure possible: porters, bearers, butlers, valets, tailors, cooks, ayahs, amahs, dhobis, water-carriers, lampmen, guards, footmen, gardeners, grass-cutters, and sweepers—the list goes on and on. The hill-station clientele was drawn from a small but powerful and dominant élite whose lifestyle was largely sustained by the cheap labour of dependent indigenous groups.

2
Penang Hill

THE island of Penang, or Pulau Pinang, lies off the coast of Province Wellesley near the northern entrance to the Strait of Malacca. A bridge connecting it to the mainland was opened in 1985. Penang (as both the island and George Town, the principal urban centre, are invariably called) is composed almost entirely of granite, has an area of approximately 294 square kilometres, and consists of a mass of dissected hills rising sharply from a narrow coastal plain. Elevation increases towards the north-central part of the island, where Western Hill (the highest point on the island) and Penang Hill are located. In spite of the word 'hill' in the name, the hill station occupies part of a narrow, steep-sided, undulating ridge whose highest elevation is about 760 metres above sea-level (Figure 1).

The present-day hill station, which extends from the vicinity of the now defunct Crag Hotel in the north to a few hundred metres beyond Fern Hill in the south, is primarily a collection of bungalows at staggered elevations, together with a hotel, a police station, a post office, a tea kiosk, a diminutive mosque, and several minor structures. The upper tier of bungalows is more or less linked by Summit Road and several footpaths. A funicular railway descends from near the top of Strawberry Hill to the lowlands close to Ayer Itam. From atop this little belvedere of empire, great vistas unfold across George Town and the shipping channel to the verdant coastal plain of Province Wellesley and Kedah to culminate in the distant blue-green mountains of the Main Range.

Penang was acquired on behalf of the English East Indian Company in 1786 by Francis Light, a private or 'country' trader long resident in the East. He called it Prince of Wales Island after the future George IV, but the name never took hold except in official contexts. Penang was primarily acquired for naval and strategic reasons, although the Company hoped that it would also

Figure 1. Penang Hill, part of the east coast lowlands, and George Town, *c*.1830. Note the topography, the waterfall, and the winding track leading up to the hill station. (Courtesy of the Map Room, British Library, London.)

serve as an entrepôt for tropical produce from the Malay Peninsula and the neighbouring archipelago.

After about 1799, the Company's earlier doubts about the importance of the island were set aside, and, in 1805, Penang was made the fourth presidency of India (the other presidencies being Bengal, Bombay, and Madras). The Company's new expectations were based mainly on several panegyrics that greatly exaggerated the natural, economic, and strategic advantages of Penang, including its potential as a naval base. But Penang soon proved a great disappointment to the Company, and, in 1826, it was combined with Malacca and Singapore to form the presidency of the Straits Settlements. Penang remained the headquarters of government until 1832, when the capital of the Straits was moved to Singapore.

Penang Hill was possibly the first imperial outpost of its kind in the British colonies because it originated in the late eighteenth century, whereas the earliest hill stations in India date from around 1820. The basic outlines of Penang Hill took shape during the first two decades of the nineteenth century, when the hill station enjoyed a brief heyday. One result of Penang's elevation to the status of a presidency in 1805 was the arrival on the island of a new, enlarged staff of civil servants and military officers, and it was mainly from this official class that there arose a demand for health-and-resort facilities on the ridge overlooking George Town. But as the total number of Europeans on the island probably did not average more than 300 in this formative period, the hill station remained small and only modestly developed. When the presidency was abolished in 1830, the Company's staff of officials and its expenditure on the island were greatly reduced, while the pool of other potential users of the hill station, like planters, merchants, and traders, remained very small. A period of stagnation ensued that lasted until the 1920s, when a funicular railway brought new life to the hill station.

Called variously Government Hill, Great Hill, or simply The Hill, the core of the early hill station occupied part of the undulating upper ridge between Fern Hill and Strawberry Hill (Figure 2). The pre-eminent hill-station site was atop Flagstaff Hill, where Bel Retiro, the governor's bungalow, was located. This

11

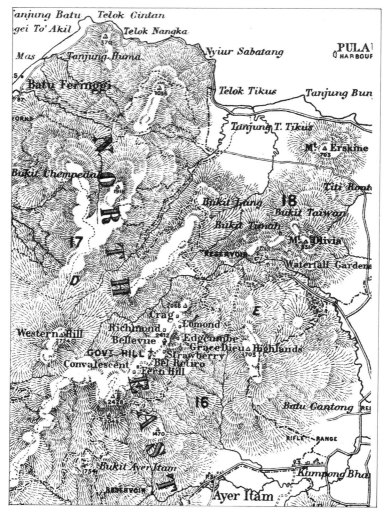

Figure 2. Penang Hill, also called variously Government Hill, Great Hill, or simply The Hill, 1897. Most of the places mentioned in the description of the hill station can be located on this map. (Courtesy of the Map Room, British Library, London.)

structure consisted of two large thatch- or *atap*-covered bungalows connected by a covered plank passage or gallery that was cool and airy when opened along the sides. A 'very large mansion, elegant and commodious, and beautifully situated with regard to salubrity' is how Dr Yvan described it in the 1850s. Towering above Bel Retiro was a flagstaff that served as a beacon or signal station (Colour Plate 2).

Near by on Mount Hygeia (named after the Greek goddess of health) accommodation for Company employees was available at Convalescent Bungalow. James Brooke, later the first rajah of Sarawak, described the view in 1830 from the bungalow as 'a landscape of vast extent, and so diversified that the eye never wearies of gazing' (Colour Plate 3 and see Cover Plate). Visitors to the island who wanted to spend a night on the hill sometimes used Convalescent Bungalow, although such a sojourn required official permission. On a neighbouring elevation stood Fern Hill (Colour Plate 4), the medical officer's residence, which had 'a dispensary and other requisites for affording aid to invalids who resort to it', according to Dr T. M. Ward's paper of 1830 on the medical topography of the island.

Slightly below and a little to the north of Bel Retiro, on what was generally called Haliburton's Hill, was the spacious bungalow of Thomas Halyburton (as his name was actually spelled), a British merchant and sometime sheriff of Prince of Wales Island. The traveller, author, and artist James Wathen described (and sketched) the view in 1811 from the bungalow looking eastward towards the mainland. He wrote that '[t]he eye, after passing over the abrupt side of the mountain, cloathed with a thick and almost impenetrable forest of gigantic trees, rests delighted on the beautiful plain, stretching from its border to the sea. This charming valley is thickly studded with handsome villas and picturesque bungalows, and intersected with pleasant carriage-roads, and meandering streams issuing from the mountains, making a reluctant passage to the sea.' A contemporary observer, Captain Robert Smith, engineer, architect, and talented amateur artist, captured part of the same view from Haliburton's Hill in one of his paintings (Colour Plate 5). The bungalow on this hill was sometimes referred to as

13

Belle Vue or Bellevue, and the hotel that now occupies its site has retained the latter form of the name.

Another commodious bungalow stood on nearby Strawberry Hill. Colonel H. G. Nahuijs van Burgst, a Dutch visitor to Penang in 1824, commented that the summit of the hill was graced by 'a shady and scented garden of roses and strawberries, whence this spot has derived its name of Strawberry Hill' (Colour Plate 6). The site of the old bungalow and gardens has been occupied for several decades by a little tea kiosk (Plate 1), below which is the upper terminus of the funicular railway. These bungalows, together with a few others about which little information has survived, were loosely connected by a tree-lined path that petered out on the summit of Western Hill, which had been cleared of forest but was not built on or cultivated.

The rounded hill immediately below the upper ridge was linked by a winding path to the track leading up to the hill station, although the bungalow there, called Highlands of Scotland, and

1. Strawberry Hill Tea Kiosk, Penang Hill, *c.*1930. The bungalow and the garden were typical PWD creations. (Courtesy of the Royal Commonwealth Society Library, London.)

14

cleared land were primarily part of the plantation economy (see Figures 1 and 2). A temporary hospital occupied the summit of this hill prior to the late 1820s, but the benefits of the hill air, according to Ward, were 'scarcely sufficient to warrant the adoption of the same measure in future'. The neighbouring hills, including Mount Olivia, the Pentlands (or Pentland Ridge), and Mount Elvira, lacked direct access to the hill station and were too low to be of much value to invalids. They occasionally served as places of refuge and resort, but functionally they were not part of the hill station.

Several additional bungalows were erected on or below the crest of the main ridge in the half-century or so after about 1830, but few other changes occurred before or indeed for some time after the completion of the funicular railway in 1923. '[It] surprised me to note,' A. L. Hoops writes in the mid-1930s, 'how few additional residences have been built on the Great Hill since Dr. Ward wrote in 1830, and how closely they are clumped near the course of the railway.' Over the years from around 1928 to 1941, however, the railway had a considerable impact on Penang Hill because, among other things, several miles of contour roads and paths were constructed and these opened up sites for new bungalows at staggered elevations; a police station, a post office, a PWD office, and several other structures were erected on or near Strawberry Hill; a reservoir and a pumping station were built on Tiger Hill; dwellings and other structures for railway employees were constructed near the railway line; several non-Europeans acquired hill-station bungalows; and the accessibility of the hill station was greatly enhanced. But how did sojourners reach the hill station prior to 1923?

Few road improvements extended beyond George Town and its immediate vicinity prior to the mid-1790s, and for another decade or more roads within the town were inadequately drained and frequently impassable. The interior of the island was then largely unexplored and mostly inaccessible, although as early as 1787 or thereabouts a rough track had been hacked through the rain forest to the signal house on the crest of the ridge overlooking George Town. Just getting to the foot of the ridge must have been a rather

difficult task before 1792 when a road was cut from the entrance
into the forest to the waterfall northwest of the town (see Figures 1
and 2). In 1795, Captain Walter Caulfield Lennon recorded in his
journal: 'This morning [I] went to see the waterfall, which is about
six miles from the town, with a road for carriages for about four of
the way, the rest I walked, and after climbing the latter part of it up
a very steep and jungly path, at last arrived at the foot of the
waterfall, and was exceedingly struck with the grandeur and
magnificence it exhibited.' It was from here, from the vicinity of
the falls, that a narrow path began a sinuous climb to the upper
ridge. Further road improvements in the late 1790s eased the journey to the falls, which soon became a favourite resort (Colour
Plate 7).

The hill station was reached in two stages: from George Town
to the foot of the ridge on horseback or by palanquin or gharry
(usually a two-wheeled carriage or cart drawn by a horse or pony
and plying for hire), and from there to the crest of the ridge by
Sumatran pony or in a sedan chair (Colour Plate 8 and Plate 2).
J. Johnson, a surgeon in the Royal Navy, described an ascent of the
ridge in 1805: 'The path-way which is not more than eight or
ten feet wide, is cut with incredible labour, through a forest of
immensely tall trees.... Steep and rugged as this path is, the little
Sumatran horses mount it with great safety: the ladies, however,
are generally carried up in a kind of sedan chair, borne on the
shoulders of stout Malays. After a tiresome ascent of two or three
hours, we gained the summit.' How tiresome too it must have
been for the 'stout Malays', not to mention the gangs of other
labourers who carried food and other supplies up to the hill station
on their backs.

Readers of N. B. Dennys's 1894 *Descriptive Dictionary of British
Malaya* were informed that '[t]he charge for a pony up the hill is
1\frac{1}{2}$, and the same for the mount down. The charge for a chair
coolie up is 35 cents, and a similar charge for the journey down.
From five to eight coolies are required for each chair, but, of
course, this is regulated by the weight of the person to be carried.
Before ascending the hill it is necessary to make arrangements with
either Messrs. Hin Lee and Co., or Boon Tek and Co., who will

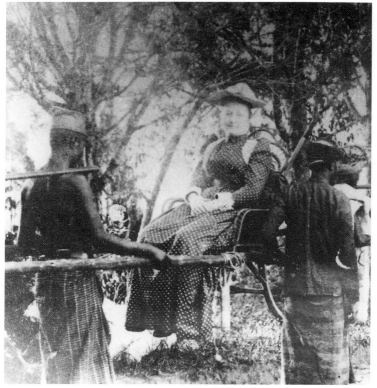

2. Victorian lady in a sedan chair, Penang, *c.*1880. Observe her enveloping attire.

provide the necessary ponies or coolies at the foot of the hill.' Sedan chairs continued to be available for hire for some time after the completion of the funicular railway, although their use was increasingly confined to the conveyance of sojourners from the Strawberry Hill terminus of the railway to the Crag Hotel (see Chapter 6).

The Penang Hills Railway was completed in 1923 (three English engineers had attempted to build a similar kind of railway in the 1890s, but the equipment they installed failed to operate).

About 2 kilometres long and rising some 726 metres above sea-level, the railway negotiated the steep gradient of the ridge in two entirely independent sections: from the lower station near Ayer Itam to a transfer station about half-way up the rise, and from there to the upper station on Strawberry Hill. The railway featured numerous viaducts and a precipitous tunnel near the top end of the line, making its construction a considerable engineering feat (Plate 3). With the opening of the hill railway, Penang Hill soon became a popular holiday resort. The number of visitors increased from 136,000 before the war to 351,000 in 1951, according to a 1952 guidebook to the island. But the hill station had not always functioned primarily as a holiday retreat.

During the nineteenth century, Penang Hill served as a refuge from the disease hazards and enervating climatic conditions of the lowlands. Penang was a very unhealthy place for several decades; and sickness occasionally reduced the number of European-born administrators to the minimum. It is fairly certain that the main causes of mortality and morbidity were malaria, tropical ulcers, diarrhoea, and dysentery. Europeans also suffered from, or were threatened by, periodic outbreaks of smallpox and cholera. Several factors were responsible for the high incidence of sickness and mortality: parts of George Town were poorly drained, dirty, and overcrowded; medical knowledge was rudimentary; hospitals were crude and unhygienic; and Europeans generally ignored the medical knowledge and adaptive behaviour of the indigenous peoples. But unlike the other Straits Settlements, Penang was blessed with a hilly interior to which invalids could repair. The benefits of such a practice can be traced to certain medical ideas.

External or environmental causes of disease were emphasized in the nineteenth century. Consequently, much attention was given to variations in temperature, wind direction, nearness to water, type of vegetation, and altitude. Many diseases were attributed to pollution of the ambient air. Localities that were low, hot, damp, and inadequately ventilated were considered especially subject to injurious miasmas. Upland areas were healthier because elevation moderated temperature and humidity, two principal reasons for vegetative decay and hence for miasmas, and were generally better ventilated than lowland areas. In short, uplands were better suited to European constitutions, which supposedly degenerated in the lowlands. All observers agreed that Penang Hill was much healthier than the inadequately ventilated lowlands on the island. Patients suffering from fever, dysentery, and hepatic diseases did very well on the hill, according to Ward, although the occurrence of fogs and mists made the hill station less suitable for pulmonary disorders and rheumatism. In *Some Glimpses into Life in the Far East* (1864), John Turnbull Thomson made a typical observation when he wrote that the air on the Great Hill was 'buoyant, cool, elevating to the spirits, bracing to the nerves, and exciting to the appetite'.

Noxious airborne odours supposedly came from native settlements, which were also thought to harbour contagious diseases like syphilis and plague. Europeans responded by restricting social intercourse with native women and by locating civil and military lines away from, and upwind of, native areas. The usually isolated, purpose-built hill station or upland military station (or cantonment) provided even greater segregation from indigenous cultures and their perceived baleful effects. Another presumed cause of disease was individual predisposition, which was related to factors such as excessive consumption of alcohol, sexual indulgence, emotional strain, and fatigue.

Penang Hill served as a convalescent station or sanatorium during the nineteenth century, although the number of sick persons who repaired to it was always very small. It was a minor place of refuge, and it supplemented rather than replaced the mineral bath and the sea or river voyage, two other well-tried means of seeking health and vitality that persisted into the twentieth century. How efficacious was Penang Hill as a refuge? A plausible answer is that the place offered psychological respite from, but had rather limited curative· effect on, the diseases that the European hill-station clientele suffered. It was too low to escape the ravages of *Anopheles maculatus*, the main vector of malaria in cleared hilly areas up to an elevation of about 1 525 metres above sea-level, and a stint on the hill probably did little for invalids who suffered from dysentery and other intestinal disorders. But there was possibly some truth in Ward's claim that the hill station's cooler air and splendid scenery

PENANG HILLS RAIL

TIME TABLE

UP TRAINS

MONDAY TO FRIDAY between 6.30 a.m. and 8-00 a.m. every half hour
    Between 8-00 a m. and 10 a.m. every qaurter hour.
    Between 10 a.m. and 4-00 p.m. every half hour.
    Between 4-00 p.m. and 6-00 p m. every quarter hour.
    Between 6-00 p m. and 7-30 p.m. every half hour.
SATURDAYS between 6-30 a.m and 8 a.m. every haif hour.
    Between 8 a m. and 10 a m every quarter hour.
    Between 10 a.m and 12 noon every half hour.
    Between 12 noon and 6-30 p.m every quarter hour.
    Between 6-30 p m. and 7-30 p.m every half hour.
SUNDAYS between 6-30 a.m. and 6-00 p m every quarter hour.
    Between 6-00 p.m. and 7-30 p.m. every half hour.

DOWN TRAINS

MONDAY TO FRIDAY between 6-45 a m. and 7-45 a.m. every half hour
    Between 7-45 a.m. and 9-45 a.m. every quarter hour.
    Between 9-45 a m and 3-45 p.m. every half hour.
    Between 3-45 p m. and 6-15 p.m. every quarter hour.
    Between 6-15 p-m and 7-15 p.m. every hal' hour
SATURDAYS between 6.45 a m. and 7-45 a m every half hour.
    Between 7-45 a m and 9-45 p.m every quarter hour.
    Between 9-45 a.m. and 12-15 p.m. every half hour.
    Between 12-15 p.m. and 6-15 p.m. every quarter hour.
    Between 6-15 p.m. and 7-15 p.m. every half hour.
SUNDAYS between 6-45 a.m. and 6.15 p.m. every quarter hour.
    Between 6-15 p m. and 7-15 p.m. every half hour.

For further particulars apply to:
Municipal Offices, Penang, ENGINE

3. Completed in 1923, the Penang Hills Railway was a considerable engineering feat. (From *Malaysia and Indo-China: Information for Visitors ...*, 1926.)

WAY

Special Trains are run on all Public Holidays.

FARES

1st CLASS ...... $ 1.00
each way.
2nd CLASS ...... 50 cts.
each way.

Children under 12 years of age half rates.

CONCESSION TICKETS (20 Rides)

1st CLASS ...... $ 10.00
2nd CLASS 5.00

SEASON TICKETS
[Monthly]

1st CLASS ...... $ 18.00
2nd CLASS 9.00

Refreshment Room near Upper Station

Journey takes only 24 minutes each way.

Penang Hill R. W. Botom Station

& MANAGER, Penang Hills Railway

were 'soothing to the mind of the invalid'.

In spite of considerable advances in medical knowledge at the turn of the twentieth century, most Europeans continued to believe that they were constitutionally unsuited to a prolonged residence in the tropics. Consequently, sojourners continued to frequent Penang Hill for a change of air, although increasingly they did so mainly to regain vigour, to escape the monotony of the equatorial climate, or to prevent sickness rather than to recover from serious physical illness.

Penang Hill was also a resort or social place from the outset (Chapter 6), although its attractions were always rather limited. When Charles Walter Kinloch ('Bengal Civilian') visited the hill station in 1852, he complained, not entirely unfairly, that anyone contemplating a lengthy stay there 'would do well to provide himself with a supply of books, for he will find neither society nor amusement on the mountain, and will be dependant [sic] solely upon his own resources for the means of filling up his time. A very few days will serve to make him acquainted with the different rides and walks of the neighbourhood; and unless he possess [sic] some resource of amusement within himself, he will probably tire of the Penang Hill in less than a week.'

3
Interlude: The British in the Malay States

UNTIL the 1870s, British rule in the Malay Peninsula was confined to the Straits Settlements. More interested in protecting trade than in acquiring territory, the British attempted to stay aloof from the affairs of the Malay states, which, for the most part, remained heavily forested, thinly populated, economically undeveloped, and largely *terra incognita* to Europeans (Colour Plate 9). In practice, however, the British found it increasingly difficult to maintain a policy of non-intervention in the Peninsular states. The quickening pace of industrialization at home whetted the appetite for raw materials and foreign markets, and the opening of the Suez Canal in 1869 proved a boon to British business interests in South-East Asia. Changing local conditions also made British intervention in the Malay states increasingly likely. For several decades, the British presence in the Straits had acted as an economic magnet to a swelling tide of mainly Chinese immigrants, many of whom quickly gravitated to parts of the western Malay states. By the 1870s, petty warfare between Malay chiefs over possession of important tin fields, violent clashes between rival Chinese secret societies over mining rights, and Malay dynastic disputes had combined to produce a state of chaos that threatened to spill over into the Straits Settlements.

The British policy of non-intervention was reversed in late 1873, and between 1874 and the late 1880s the four states of Perak, Selangor, Negri Sembilan, and Pahang became British protectorates. In 1895, all four states were brought together to form the Federated Malay States (FMS) with Kuala Lumpur as the capital. The remaining five states of Perlis, Kedah, Kelantan, Trengganu, and Johore, which became known, in a curiously negative sense, as the Unfederated Malay States (UMS), were induced to accept British advisers, and by 1914, British rule had been extended over the entire Peninsula.

The British forward movement paved the way for economic

development in the western Malay states, which soon emerged as the dynamic hub of the economy. After about 1880, the colonial government began to establish the framework for a profitable export economy based on tin and plantation agriculture. The main goal of the government was to establish an economic edifice in which private enterprise could flourish. Tin mining was already well established in parts of the western lowlands when the British arrived on the scene, and it was here, especially in the tin-rich states of Perak and Selangor, that economic development proceeded most rapidly. Until about 1914, most of the government's revenue was derived from the export duty on tin, and the bulk of this revenue was ploughed back into building railways and roads both within and between the main mining districts. The tin-mining economy stimulated the growth of new urban places like Kuala Lumpur and Ipoh, enhanced the demand for foodstuffs, and was accompanied by a major improvement in the transportation system, which in itself was no mean achievement in a region then dominated by primary rain forest (Plate 4).

The development of commercial agriculture was also a high priority of the colonial government, whose promotion of this enterprise came in several forms: generous loans were made to pioneer planters; experimental agricultural stations were established; land was made available on very liberal terms; new roads, tracks, and bridges were built in hitherto inaccessible areas; and migrant labour was brought in. As a result of these and other measures, planters were well positioned to take advantage of the new commercial enterprise that presented itself in the form of rubber, whose cultivation spread like wildfire in the first two decades of the twentieth century.

The policies of the colonial government resulted in the division of the Peninsula into two very different parts: an economically developed west coast lowland zone, and an economically underdeveloped eastern zone. The vital economic hub of the Peninsula was firmly established in the western lowlands facing the Strait of Malacca. It was here, especially in the Straits Settlements and the western federated states, that the great majority of the potential hill-station clientele was concentrated, and it was along the interior

4. Railway construction was greatly hampered by the wet climate and primary rain forest. (From Pat Barr, *Taming the Jungle*, 1977.)

highlands of this zone that several hill stations were developed. In the early days of British rule, however, the highlands were inaccessible.

The British intervened in a world of water transport where for millennia the seas, the straits, and the rivers had served as natural highways. There were jungle tracks and paths in some areas but these were mere adjuncts to the rivers, the main arteries of movement on the mainland. Overland travel was hampered by the dense, illimitable forest, and by the rugged topography of the interior. When that most indefatigable of Victorian lady travellers, Isabella Bird, visited the Peninsula in 1879, she found that the only way to get around parts of Perak was by elephant (Plate 5), and for some time thereafter senior British officials usually took to a boat when they went on tour (Plate 6).

Colonial authorities encouraged trade and private enterprise by investing public funds in railways and roads. The rail network was developed in three stages: first, between 1885 and 1895 four short

5. Isabella Bird on her Malayan travels, 1879. (From *The Golden Chersonese*, 1883.)

6. A British official's boat. There were few good roads in Malaya until the late nineteenth century. (From J. F. A. McNair, *Perak and the Malays*, 1878.)

lines were built in Perak, Selangor, and Negri Sembilan, each connecting an inland mining town to a port; second, between 1896 and 1910 the inland mining centres were connected by a trunk line that was further extended northwards and southwards; and third, in the period to 1931 the rail network, including the East Coast line, was completed (Figure 3). By 1923, there was through communication from Singapore to Bangkok.

The earliest roads in the Malay states were bridle paths and cart tracks that served as feeder roads linking tin-mining districts to rivers and later to railheads. By the turn of the century, a north–south trunk road extended from Malacca to Province Wellesley, and in 1898, a trans-mountain cart road was completed as far as Kuala Lipis in Pahang. Bullock or oxen carts quickly replaced elephants and human porters as the main means of hauling goods, while passenger conveyances that plied for hire, such as hackneys (Plate 7), gharries, and jinrickshaws, came into their own in the towns. The road system expanded rapidly after the introduction of the motor car at the turn of the century, and before long

Figure 3. This rather curious piece of cartography appeared in Ashley Gibson's *The Malay Peninsula and Archipelago* (1928). Note the railway network, part of which was still under construction in Kelantan.

7. Hackney carriages plied for hire in the towns. (Postcard, courtesy of Major David Ng.)

Malaya's roads were among the best in the empire. In 1907, there were sufficient motorists in Perak to form the Perak Motor Union, and by 1912, readers of the *Illustrated London News* were informed that 'the Malay Peninsula offers a new field for the motorist. Almost any make of car is suitable for a tour in Malaya. There are nearly 3000 miles of road open for the motor-car. They are magnificently constructed, mostly with easy gradients, and pass through unrivalled tropical scenery. In the principal towns there are garages with trained mechanics, and petrol is always available at convenient centres.' The car became the prime vehicle of leisure, not so much because its use collapsed physical distances, but rather because its owner gained some freedom of choice over the use of time.

It was only after the main overland lines of communication had been laid down and the basic structure of the settlement system had been established that a handful of potential hill-station sites became more accessible along the rugged spinal column of the Peninsula. However, two conditions still posed problems: first, the transportation system skirted rather than served the highlands; and second, since the highland zone was very thinly populated (its principal inhabitants were scattered groups of Senoi-speaking shifting cultivators, mainly Semai and Temiar), any new settlement there would necessarily be dependent on access to external, namely lowland, sources of food, supplies, and labour. When demand for hill stations arose, these problems were solved by building roads that 'tapped into' the main transportation network. The three main connections, all of them dead-end roads, were from near Taiping to Maxwell's Hill (this link was more like a track than a road), from Tapah to Cameron Highlands, and from near the Gap rest-house, on the main Kuala Lumpur–Kuantan road, to Fraser's Hill. But before these roads were built there had to be a demand for hill stations, so let us look briefly at how this came about.

British intervention in the Malay states resulted in rapid population growth from about 1880. Immigration was actively encouraged by the colonial government, which considered an expanded labour force to be essential to economic growth. Consequently, there was a massive influx of Chinese and Indians and a great increase in the flow of immigrants from various parts of the Malay Archipelago. The number of Europeans in the Peninsula also increased substantially. Between 1891 and 1931, for example, the European population of the Straits Settlements grew from 4,422 to 10,003 while that of the FMS (formed in 1895) increased from 719 to 6,350 (of which Pahang accounted for only 390). On the other hand, there were only 1,295 Europeans in the UMS in 1931. Like the great majority of other immigrants, Europeans gravitated to the western lowlands, where they were mainly concentrated in the cities of Singapore and Kuala Lumpur and in the states of Perak and Selangor—in other words, in the major commercial and administrative centres and in the main planting and mining areas. The British comprised the great majority of the Europeans, and most of the British were English.

The Europeans were divided into so-called officials and unofficials, the distinction being between those who worked for the government and those who were privately employed. The former included civil servants as well as the professional and technical staffs of governmental departments, while the latter included

30

planters, miners, and businessmen. Both components of the European community grew rapidly after the turn of the century, but it
was the unofficials who recorded the more spectacular growth,
thanks largely to the widespread adoption of rubber cultivation.

It was not until after World War I that there was any appreciable
increase in the number of women in the European community.
The social historian John Butcher attributes their growing presence in the FMS to the arrival there of a larger proportion of mar-
ried men, adjustments in civil service salaries that made it easier for
men to marry, and the fact that 'living conditions were now considered much more suitable, though still far from ideal, for
European women than they had been previously. By about 1920
the threat of malaria had been greatly reduced. In the smaller
towns Europeans had clubs, cold storage, and other amenities
which earlier had only been found in the main towns.' Although
the great majority of European women who came to Malaya did so
as wives, many soon found themselves periodically separated from
their husbands and children. This situation arose from certain prevailing views of the deleterious health effects of the tropical climate, most notably the widely held belief that children and women
'deteriorated' more rapidly than did men in the low latitudes.
Consequently, children were usually not kept in Malaya beyond
the age of five or six, when they were sent home to be educated,
and it was generally expected that women, who sometimes went
home with their children, would spend less time in the tropics than
their husbands.

British rule in Malaya was based more on prestige than on military force. Europeans preserved their prestige by maintaining
among themselves a higher standard of living than that enjoyed by
other cultural groups, and by staying aloof from the alien world all
around. As in their other colonies, the British in Malaya ruled in
enclave. Separateness was a technique of dominance. Part of that
separateness or aloofness was reflected, for example, in the importance that was attached to social clubs and hill stations. Europeans
in the FMS came primarily from the middle class and comprised
a remarkably homogeneous community in Malaya. The cultural
baggage that representatives of this community brought to the

Peninsula included a shared predilection for a certain residential style of life, for certain forms of recreation and leisure, and for certain specialized kinds of social and recreational places.

The demand for hill stations on the mainland arose in the 1880s and grew thereafter as the European population increased. There were two main reasons for this demand. First in importance was the socio-cultural background and experiences of the Europeans themselves. Their socially and culturally prescribed behavioural patterns included a preference for spending a few weeks each year at a resort, ostensibly for health reasons but also certainly for recreational and social reasons. In short, there was a demand in Malaya for specialized social places that would serve as the tropical equivalents of the metropolitan resorts. The second reason for the demand was related to the perceived baleful effects of long residence in the mephitic and pestiferous tropical lowlands, combined with the alleged physical and psychological benefits of periodic sojourns in the cool and bouyant air of the hills.

Certain more specific characteristics of the colonial community in Malaya also gave rise to the demand. First, Europeans sought places where they could be by themselves and where they could escape from the alien land and life of the lowlands. Hill stations were like social clubs writ large: they were enclaves of racial and social segregation. Second, it was expensive and time-consuming to journey to the higher latitudes of home, and the opportunity to do so arose only infrequently. There was therefore a demand for substitute temperate places that were readily accessible. And third, hill stations conjured up prospects of family togetherness. As Butcher notes, children 'could receive at least the early years of their education at a hill school.... Women would be able to spend some of their time with their husbands in the lowlands and some with their children in the highlands. Whole families could be together during holidays and for the few weeks a year when men had local leave.' For the most part, however, these three considerations were related to, rather than separate from, the two main reasons behind the demand for hill stations.

4
The Mainland Belvederes

THE relief of the north-central part of the Peninsula features a number of roughly parallel, more or less north–south aligned mountain ranges with granitic cores. The longest and most prominent of these ranges—indeed, the most impressive physical feature in the landscape—is the Central or Main Range, which extends continuously from the Thai border to Negri Sembilan and contains most of the Peninsula's mountain peaks with elevations above 1 500 metres. It was on this rugged spinal column of the Peninsula, or on rib-like offshoots from it, that the British built several hill stations from the 1880s to the 1930s.

Four tiny belvederes that were intended primarily for the use of officials were established by state governments in the 1880s and 1890s: Maxwell's Hill (as the scatter of bungalows above Taiping came to be called) and Gunong Kledang in Perak, Bukit Kutu in Selangor, and Gunong Angsi in Negri Sembilan. The latter three could boast only five bungalows between them. Maxwell's Hill was somewhat larger, but like the others its growth was hampered by a lack of flat land for building sites. The rapid increase in the European-born population of the Peninsula after about 1900 was accompanied by a growing demand for more and bigger hill stations, and for some years there was great interest in a pre-World War I proposal to develop a grand highland outpost on the south side of Gunong Tahan in Pahang. That scheme was eventually abandoned, and it was not until the 1920s and 1930s that two more substantial hill stations were eventually developed: Fraser's Hill and Cameron Highlands (see Endpapers).

Three Tiny Hill Stations

The 1902 *Handbook of the Federated Malay States* claims that Perak was 'well provided with the means of recruiting health by a change to cool air from the torrid atmosphere of the plains'. This reference was to its 'sanitaria', which included Gunong Kledang, situated some 13 kilometres from Ipoh and rising about 805 metres above sea-level, where a bungalow had been erected in 1892 and another in 1902. This diminutive belvedere was reached in two stages: from Ipoh to the foot of the hill by a good cart road, and from there to the bungalows by a well-maintained bridle path that permitted 'the use of riding horses, or of chairs carried by coolies for the benefit of those for whom active exercise is undesirable', according to the handbook.

In 1895, the Selangor government erected a bungalow of granite and timber on Bukit Kutu, a western offshoot of the Main Range above the old town of Kuala Kubu, and a second bungalow went up in 1904–5. Visitors to Bukit Kutu—also called Treacher's Hill after W. H. Treacher, who climbed the hill in 1893 to investigate its suitability as a resort—enjoyed an extensive view from the hilltop and a relatively dry climate. Mrs Stratton-Brown describes a visit to Bukit Kutu in the 1890s:

'For a big holiday Bukit Kubu ... was the choice. One went by rail to the terminus at Kuala Kubu, [then] walked, rode or was carried seven miles to the top of the hill by jungle track to a nice bungalow. Usually two families applied for leave. One for the first fortnight (the time permitted for use of the bungalow by Government) and the other for the second, and so the women part of the families had a month with their children—the men folk getting a fortnight. Of course one had to take provisions. On one of the expeditions on which I went, two sheep were driven up, crates of fowls, ducks etc. carried by coolies, all tinned provisions in boxes. One took one's houseboy, and, if there were children, amahs or ayahs. It needed some 20 coolies for the baggage, so it became a minor mountaineering proposition. Most of us walked the whole way but the older women and babies were carried in chairs slung from poles, four carriers to a chair.... We left Kuala Lumpur by the early morning train, got to Kuala Kubu station about 9 am, had breakfast at the resthouse [Plate 8], and then went ... uphill on jungle tracks, single file.... [The bungalow had] four big bedrooms and a dining room and living room, kitchen and servants' quarters. Fires were lighted, for it was chilly.... There was a tennis court

8. The rest-house at Kuala Kubu. Travellers from Kuala Lumpur often stopped here on their way to Fraser's Hill. (Courtesy of Antiques of the Orient, Singapore.)

marked out and fresh vegetable plots were looked after by the caretaker and his mate.'

Bukit Kutu has been a wildlife reserve since 1922. The hill station was destroyed during the Japanese Occupation and was not rebuilt, and the old track to Kuala Kubu was long ago reclaimed by the rain forest.

Gunong Angsi in Negri Sembilan was a diminutive highland outpost with a single bungalow at an elevation of about 800 metres above sea-level. A winding path led up to the bungalow, which consisted of six bedrooms, two bathrooms, a dining-room, and narrow front and back verandas. A. Hale wrote in *Twentieth Century Impressions of British Malaya* (1908), that a 'bungalow has been built at Sri Memengok, on Gunong Angsi, at an elevation of 2,626 feet. The main [railway] line goes through the pass between Rembau and Sungei Ujong near the foot of Gunong Angsi, and the flag-station at Perhentian Tinggi is only four and a half miles from the bungalow, making this the most easily reached of all the hill-stations at present.' Reflecting on his experiences in Negri Sembilan during the 1930s, Sjovald Cunyngham-Brown recalled in his *Crowded Hour* that there used to be a hill station called

Gunong Angsi and that his mother was conveyed there from Perhentian Tinggi 'by sedan-chair one Christmas to form the nucleus of a memorable family party'.

Negri Sembilan also had the little seaside resort of Port Dickson, which was readily accessible by road, rail, and steamer. There were facilities there for sea bathing, and the air was thought to be peculiarly dry and salubrious. The 1935 *Handbook to British Malaya* commented that an 'enjoyable holiday may be spent at Port Dickson ... where rooms at the Sanatorium or a Government bungalow, of which there are six, may be obtained on application to the Lady Supervisor of Government Bungalows'.

After about 1905, senior government officials began to show considerable interest in the possibility of developing a grand hill station on the south side of 2 187 metre-high Gunong Tahan in northern Pahang, the Peninsula's highest mountain. The scheme called for two railways: one branching off from the proposed line to Kelantan (see Figure 3), the other a funicular railway up the mountain to the hill-station site on a high plateau. The suitability of Gunong Tahan for an upland outpost was confirmed in 1912 when the mountain was climbed by an exploratory party that included the then Governor of the Straits Settlements, Sir Arthur Young. In the same year, Arnold Wright and Thomas Reid commented in *The Malay Peninsula* that a Gunong Tahan hill station would mean 'life and health for hundreds, who, in the absence of such a convenient health resort, would have either to be invalided to Europe or compelled to recuperate in some expensive resort in Java or Ceylon'. The project, however, was never begun, probably for a combination of three reasons: the relative distance of northern Pahang from the more populous parts of the west coast lowlands, the enormous expense of the proposed railways, and the political difficulties surrounding the fact that the northern side of Gunong Tahan was in Kelantan, which was not in the FMS.

1. Street scene, Simla, summer capital of the Raj and the imperial belvedere *par excellence*. (Postcard)

2. Bel Retiro and neighbouring bungalows, 1856. Note the form of the *atap*-covered bungalows, the deep verandas, and the bamboo screens (*chiks*). Water-colour by Captain Charles Henry Cazalet. (Courtesy of Dr George Yuille Caldwell.)

3. View from Convalescent Bungalow, Prince of Wales Island, c.1818. Aquatint by William Daniell, 1821. (Courtesy of the Museum & Art Gallery, Penang.)

4. Fern Cottage, 1847. Penang Hill's luxuriant vegetation was a major attraction to most sojourners. Water-colour by

5. Admiring the view from Haliburton's Hill, c.1818. Note the servant holding a parasol, the clothing of the two European men, and the extensive green sward. Aquatint by William Daniell, 1821. (Courtesy of the Museum & Art Gallery, Penang.)

6. View from Strawberry Hill, c.1818. The large tree was probably a remnant of the original rain forest. Observe the pineapples and the sunflowers in the flower-bed, the green sward with scattered shrubs, and the clothing of the two European women. Aquatint by William Daniell, 1821. (Courtesy of the Museum & Art Gallery, Penang.)

7. The waterfall north-west of George Town was a favourite resort. Lithograph by Admiral Theodore-Auguste Fisquet, *c.*1836–7. (Courtesy of Datuk Lim Chong Keat.)

8. Journey up the hill and glimpses of life at the top. Pen-and-wash by Jackson (attributed), 1863.

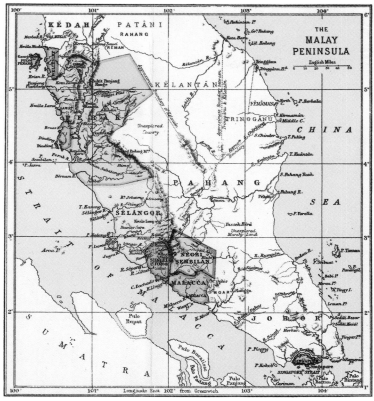

9. Large parts of the interior of the Malay Peninsula remained unknown to Europeans until the early decades of the twentieth century. (From Isabella Bird, *The Golden Chersonese*, 1883.)

10. Penang, from Richmond Hill, *c.*1850. Note the form and siting of the bungalow (*left foreground*) and the demarcated compound with scattered shrubs. Lithograph by W. Spreat. (From 'Bengal Civilian' [Charles Walter Kinloch], *Rambles in Java and the Straits in 1852*, 1853.)

11. The Waterfall (or Botanic) Garden, c.1917. Established in 1884, the garden soon became a favourite resort. (Postcard, courtesy of Major David Ng.)

12. Mrs F. B-P watching ships in Penang Harbour, c.1858. Water-colour by Captain Frederick Bannerman-Phillips. (Courtesy of Datuk Lim Chong Keat.)

13. A European couple relaxing in the grounds of the Crag Hotel, c.1908. (Postcard, courtesy of Major David Ng.)

14. Crag Hotel, c.1908. Bungalows and shady walks. (Postcard, courtesy of Major David Ng.)

15. Looking out to sea from Maxwell's Hill. (From Philip C. Coote, *Peeps at Many Lands*, 1923.)

16. A room in Woodlands, Penang Hill, c.1858. Note the metropolitan-style décor and the clothing of the two European women. Water-colour by Captain Frederick Bannerman-Phillips. (Courtesy of Datuk Lim Chong Keat.)

Maxwell's Hill

The earliest hill station on the mainland was situated on the Larut Hills of Perak, overlooking the mining and administrative centre of Taiping, which was widely regarded as the most picturesque town in the Peninsula. During her visit there in 1879, Bird stayed at the British Residency (Plate 9), whose occupant at that time was Assistant Resident William Edward Maxwell (Plate 10), after whom the hill station was eventually named.

Several bungalows were erected on the hills above Taiping in the 1880s. The first to go up was The Cottage, built in 1884 for the Resident of Perak (it was later the bungalow of the chief administrator of the FMS, variously called Resident-General, Chief Secretary, Federal Secretary, in that order). Three bungalows were erected for the use of Perak government officers: The Tea

9. A wet day at the British Residency, Larut, Perak. Note the chairs with the long leg-rests. (From *The Graphic*.)

Gardens and Maxwell's Hill in 1887, and The Hut (Plate 11) in 1889. Early printed sources refer to the bungalows as 'sanitaria', and in his 1898 book, Ambrose Rathborne noted that 'a sanatorium was made by building several bungalows ... where many an invalid has since been restored to health'. Two other early hill-station bungalows were The Box and The Nest. Built in 1887, the former was the bungalow of the British Resident of Perak (by that time The Cottage was the Resident-General's residence), while the latter was a private bungalow owned by the American Methodist Mission.

10. W. E. Maxwell (1846–97), after whom Maxwell's Hill was named. (From Walter Makepeace, Gilbert E. Brooke, and Roland St. J. Braddell, *One Hundred Years of Singapore*, Vol. 2, 1921.)

The early hill station also featured a post office, quarters for the Superintendent of Government Plantations, and clearings for a vegetable-and-flower garden and a herd of cattle, both government-owned. Tea was experimented with for a while (hence The Tea Gardens) but this project failed and the tea gardens were converted into pastures for cattle. The experimental botanist Leonard Wray was the superintendent of the hill station in the early days, and there, according to Barr, he 'experimented with the growing of European vegetables and homely flowers such as begonias and gloxinas sent from Mr Bull of Chelsea—which gladdened the eyes of the officers suffering from debilitating fevers who had come up to recuperate, and their wives who drifted along the leafy lanes collecting wild ferns and orchids'.

Although three of the bungalows were intended primarily for the use of public officers, the *Perak Handbook and Civil Service List* of 1893 was careful to point out that 'any application made on the ground of ill-health, supported by medical certificate, may at any

11. The Hut, Maxwell's Hill, late 1890s. The lady in the garden is
Mrs Treacher, the wife of W. H. Treacher, Resident of Perak. (Courtesy
of Arkib Negara, Kuala Lumpur.)

time be accepted as giving the first claim'. The handbook went on
to say that linens, towels, and blankets were not supplied at the
bungalows, that two or three 'mountain chairs' in the charge of the
PWD were available for the conveyance of invalids (in later years
this service was provided by the local firm of Taik Ho and
Company), and that Chinese shopkeepers in Taiping would will-
ingly 'arrange with visitors for sending up daily supplies at a reasonable cost', presumably by horse or pony. Unlike Penang Hill,
this hill station produced some of its own needs, notably vegetables, flowers, milk, and butter, small quantities of which were
'exported' to the lowlands.

The future of Maxwell's Hill looked very bright to Hale in 1907
when he observed that all that was required to popularize it was
'the erection of a good hotel and the establishment of a pony or
mule service for riding and a bullock service for transport of baggage, failing, of course, the construction of a mountain railway. All

these things will come in time, as the States become more populated with Europeans.' But these hoped-for-things did not come in time. Instead, access remained difficult, no hotel was built, and the European community clamoured for bigger and better hill stations. The major problem with Maxwell's Hill was that it lacked flat land for further growth and development. It never acquired more than about ten bungalows, and its production of flowers and foods remained insignificant.

Fraser's Hill

Fraser's Hill got its name from Louis James Fraser, sometime resident of Tras, where he ran a transport service by mule between Kuala Kubu and Raub, and later of Bukit Fraser, as the hill was originally called, where he built himself a bungalow (Plate 12) and engaged in tin mining around the turn of the century. A company later took over his property, and the legendary Fraser apparently died sometime in the early 1900s. J. H. M. Robson recalled that he 'looked a frail old man and had some slight disfigurement to one

12. Louis James Fraser's bungalow, c.1918. (From *Malaya*, September 1952.)

eye. But he was much tougher than he looked. On one occasion his Malay attendants thought he was dead and actually started to bury him. Luckily the corpse came to life again before it was too late.'

A rough path some 8–10 kilometres long linked Bukit Fraser to the Gap near the highest point on the cross-mountain trunk road between Selangor and Pahang. There was a rest-house at the Gap, and this little place served as a health resort in the early days. It was, as Hale pointed out, a convenient place to stop because 'the Federal motor-buses and cars, running every day, pass the door' (Plate 13). No doubt another attraction was the lovely rose garden that graced the spot. The Bishop of Singapore, C. J. Ferguson-Davie, spent a short holiday at the Gap rest-house in November 1917, a date that marked the turning point in the history of Fraser's Hill.

The Bishop and his holiday companion, A. B. Champion, then Chaplain of Selangor, climbed Bukit Fraser early one morning, then spent the rest of the day searching for possible bungalow sites on the ridges of the hill and above the valley where the golf course was later laid out. On his return to Singapore, the Bishop wrote a report to the government suggesting that Bukit Fraser could be rapidly and cheaply developed as a hill station. This was welcome news in 1917, because for several years the seemingly endless world war had made it virtually impossible for Europeans to go home on leave. Denied access to the higher latitudes of home, Europeans looked instead to the Main Range, whence they hoped help would come in the form of a new change-of-air station. By the end of the war, the government had decided to go ahead with the development of Bukit Fraser as a hill station.

A topographical survey of the hill-station site was conducted in 1918, and work began on the access road from the Gap in 1919. In 1920, George Maxwell, then Chief Secretary to Government, appointed a federal Development Committee to oversee the orderly development of the hill station. Meanwhile, building sites were cleared of jungle and provided with access paths and roads, the first bungalows started to go up, and work began on preparing the site of the future golf course (Plates 14a–b). In 1921, the name

13. The Auto Mail Service plying the highway. (Courtesy of Antiques of the Orient, Singapore.)

14 a–b. The golf course at Fraser's Hill, October 1921 (*above*) and *c*.1952 (*below*). (From *Malaya*, October 1952.)

'Fraser's Hill', rather than Bukit Fraser, was chosen for the new hill station, and in 1922 the metalled access road from the Gap (with control gates at each end to regulate a one-way traffic system) was completed.

Development proceeded apace, as the following extract from the 1927 *Handbook to British Malaya* reveals: 'There are nine Government Bungalows, intended primarily for government servants.... In addition, from Red Cross funds, four houses have been built, of which two are primarily for ex-Service men and women.... Three private houses have been completed, and the construction of others is in hand. A "Country Club" in connection with the Selangor Club, Kuala Lumpur, has been inaugurated on Fraser's Hill. There is also a golf course. The water supply has been completed....' By 1930, Fraser's Hill could boast a total of sixty-three bungalows (some of these were probably minor structures), of which sixteen were privately owned, and the development of the settlement had been more or less completed.

The hill station covered an area of approximately 140 hectares (including the 16-hectare, 9-hole golf course) and had some 50 kilometres of well-kept jungle paths. It also had a boarding school for European children run by a Mrs Davidson, who had fifteen boys and girls in her charge, according to the *Planter* in 1934, and an experimental dairy farm that was located some 300 metres below the general level of the residential area.

The traveller at Fraser's Hill in the 1930s could obtain both food and accommodation at the hill-station rest-house (Plate 15) for an inclusive charge of $7.10 per diem per person. A government-owned bungalow could be rented for $4.50 per day, while rooms in that kind of bungalow cost $2.10 per day. (Charges were in Straits dollars. The exchange rate was one Straits dollar to sterling 2s. 4d. or US40–60 cents in pre-World War II terms.) The FMS Railways conducted a luggage delivery service to Fraser's Hill from its station at Kuala Kubu Road, and cars were available for hire from a private firm in Kuala Kubu Bahru.

Although it was an enjoyable experience for most visitors, Fraser's Hill did not please everyone. Some officials found its atmosphere rather too official, government-like, and stuffy, while

15. The rest-house at Fraser's Hill, *c*.1930. (Postcard, courtesy of Major David Ng.)

unofficials complained that the government's policy of reserving hill-station accommodation primarily for its own employees was unfair and discriminatory because the area had been developed with public funds. Besides, it soon became apparent to all that the hill station's cramped and constricted site could not accommodate further growth. As the demand for upland resort facilities continued to grow, the focus of interest shifted to Cameron Highlands.

Cameron Highlands

William Cameron, a government surveyor, explored the highlands due east of Batu Gajah, Perak, around 1885, but it is most un-likely that he ever saw the region that came to be called Cameron Highlands. (Until about 1933, the preferred name was Cameron's Highlands.) Before Cameron's time, the region was probably known only to groups of Senoi-speaking shifting cultivators (Plate 16). In 1885, Sir Hugh Low, British Resident of Perak, suggested that the Highlands, which were believed to include an extensive plateau, might be suitable for a health-and-pleasure resort or for farming and gardening, but these prescient ideas initially came to nothing. Nevertheless, some desultory interest was shown in penetrating the region, and by 1904, a bridle path some 55 kilometres long had been extended from Tapah to well within the Highlands. It was only in the 1920s, however, that the area's potential for development began to receive attention.

H. C. Robinson, Director of Museums, led an expedition to the Highlands in 1922, and this was followed, in 1925, by an expedition headed by Sir George Maxwell that reported on the climate, topography, health conditions, soil, geology, and other characteristics of the region. Maxwell was favourably impressed by

16. A group of Orang Asli (aborigines) near Cameron Highlands, c.1925. The young women probably belonged to the Senoi-speaking Semai or Temiar. (From *British Malaya*, 1927.)

the Highlands' potential for agricultural development and by the suitability of the place—its configuration, he wrote, 'would appear to be not unlike that of Newara [*sic*] Eliya in Ceylon and of Baguio in the Philippine Islands'—for a hill station. The immediate result of the expedition was the creation, in 1926, of the Cameron's Highlands Development Committee to oversee the planning and orderly development of the area.

Something of the optimism surrounding this new venture can be gained from an entry in the 1927 *Handbook to British Malaya*, which stated that the Highlands were situated in the upper reaches of the Bertam River in Pahang, where, as 'far as is known at present there are about 12 square miles of undulating plateau at a height of 3,500 to 4,500 feet, suitable for growing tea and economic cultivation of varied nature; and a further six or more square miles at an altitude of 4,700 to 5,200 feet eminently suitable for residential urban requirements.... There is little doubt that, if means of ready access are provided, a hill-station would be self developing.... Such a station ... would be suitable for a public school, for a seat of Government, for barracks, and so forth, and might even provide the European (as at Ootacamund and other places) with a suitable home on his retirement. It would ... spell Health at a minimum cost to the great controlling population of the country, for whom health is now a perpetual gamble, and a reasonable length of days problematical.'

The development of the Highlands was supervised and directed by the Development Committee from 1926 to 1931, when control of the project was handed over to the Pahang government. During those years, the metalled road from Tapah to the Highlands was completed, some of the larger tea estates were established, an agricultural station for experimental work was opened at Tanah Rata, and areas were set aside for agricultural, administrative, military, residential, and recreational purposes. Although the Highlands proved to have much less flat land than they were originally thought to possess, their many ridges, spurs, knolls, and other eminences provided numerous ideal sites for bungalows.

Following the completion of the main road, the government constructed access roads and paths, cleared jungle from future development sites, installed a water-supply system, and built a rest-house. Most of the subsequent development of the Highlands was carried out by private interests, and by about 1935, the region had some 280 hectares under tea cultivation, mainly British- or European-owned, a number of mostly Chinese family-run vegetable smallholdings, some fifty privately owned dwellings, two private schools for European children up to the age of about thirteen, and three hotels.

5
Bungalows and Gardens

MALAYA'S hill stations were essentially rather modest collections of bungalows, each set in its own carefully demarcated compound that also provided space for associated outbuildings and a garden. The two main influences on the bungalow-compound ensemble were the suburban ideology of the rising middle class in the metropolitan society and the residential experience of the European colonial community in India. As already mentioned, no other building or construction was more redolent of the colonial presence than the bungalow. Both the name and form of this adaptable house-type—it served not only as private dwelling but also, for example, as rest-house, hotel, club, and district office—originated in India, where the Europeans there apparently adopted and adapted the indigenous huts of rural Bengal to accord with their own social and cultural preferences.

The residential style of life of the European colonial community in Malaya was also greatly influenced by developments in the metropolitan society. Particularly important were the residential aspirations of the rising middle class because, as already noted, most of the Europeans who came to Malaya were drawn from that class. Following its introduction into England from India in the mid-nineteenth century, the bungalow idea was realized in the seaside resorts and, among other places, in the suburbs of the expanding towns and cities. By the end of the century, the majority of middle-class urbanites in England lived in suburban-style areas where the detached bungalow in its own compound had become the basic residential unit. Furthermore, suburban life was imbued with preferences and values such as a strong commitment to, or belief in, private property, privacy, fresh air and space, family life, and leisure activities like gardening. The middle-class dwelling itself was expected to house one nuclear family and to have its own specialized rooms for sleeping, eating, cooking, relaxing, and bathing.

A bungalow in early nineteenth-century Penang was a hill dwelling for temporary use by Europeans. The term at that time apparently was rarely applied to lowland dwellings, which were usually called 'houses' or 'residences'. The hill dwellings, on the other hand, were invariably referred to as bungalows, and no doubt significantly Wathen referred to one in 1811 as a commodious dwelling 'of that class'—in other words, a distinctive type of dwelling. A splendid description of Penang dwellings appeared in an 1828 issue of the *Oriental Herald and Journal of General Literature* under the heading 'Letters from the East—Penang'. There, following a brief description of Convalescent Bungalow (Plate 17), the anonymous author explained that the term 'bungalow' was reserved for 'a slighter, less lofty, and more temporary erection, than that known as a house', and that generally bungalows 'are hastily run up, are confined to a ground floor, and are constructed of wood and leaves'.

Company bungalows with names of English, Scottish, or literary provenance pre-empted the scenically most attractive and airy sites on the upper ridge above George Town. Social status and elevation were in tandem: the governor's bungalow, Bel Retiro (see Colour Plate 2), occupied the most commanding site atop the hill, with the bungalows of lesser officials and merchants below. Several of the bungalows, including Convalescent Bungalow, were relatively small.

The bungalows were low, one-storey buildings that were oblong or square in shape. They sat on slightly raised plinths or on low brick pillars (see Plate 17). They had mud or woven-mat walls, pyramidal *atap*-covered roofs, and all-round deep verandas supported by slender wooden posts. Ward mentioned that they were equipped with glass windows against the vicissitudes of the weather, and the verandas were protected from heat and glare by split green-bamboo screens or *chicks* that could be rolled up when not in use (see Colour Plate 2). Internally, they probably comprised an open central area that was used for lounging and dining, with bedrooms opening off on either side. Intended for temporary

17. Convalescent Bungalow (*right*) and Bel Retiro with its flagstaff (*left*). Note the terraced garden to the right of Bel Retiro, the plinth on which Convalescent Bungalow rested, the building materials, and the servants. (From Captain R. Elliott, *Views in India, China, and on the Shores of the Red Sea ...*, Vol. 2, 1835.)

occupation, the bungalows were only partially furnished.

Each bungalow was set in a spacious compound that was de-marcated by fences of linked hurdles or screens of trees and shrubs to ensure privacy and seclusion (Colour Plate 10). A large area around each bungalow was cleared of vegetation and allotted to a garden, servants' quarters, and a kitchen; the open space also admitted light and allowed ventilation. The result was a privately controlled, more or less self-contained milieu that was largely sus-tained and maintained by the labour and services of dependent Asians.

Linkages between Penang and Madras were especially strong, and it would appear that the form of the early Penang Hill bunga-lows was probably introduced from that part of India, as suggested by Wathen in his comment that 'the garden-houses and bungalows are erected here in the same manner, and with similar materials, as they are near Madras, with the exception of their being elevated here to avoid the floods', and by Ward in his telling observation that dwellings occupied by Europeans in the interior of the island were 'in distinct enclosures or compounds, like the garden houses at Madras, or the houses of the good citizens of London, near the metropolis'. Although the bungalow in Penang was of Indian ori-gin, it is possible that certain of its features may have been derived from the local Malay house, but available information permits only a very tentative conclusion that the Malay stilt house of timber and *atap* with a pyramidal roof and a gallery along one or more sides may have influenced the bungalow form. Some early European arrivals in Penang adopted the Malay house, but a sketch of one by Wathen in 1811 shows it to be different from the bungalow in both size and proportions.

Some of Penang Hill's bungalows eventually acquired an overlay of fashionable architectural details, while others were replaced by more substantial structures, including a few of two storeys. The old bungalow on Strawberry Hill was replaced by a bungalow that served as a tea kiosk (see Plate 1). Both the form of this building and the composition of its surrounding garden were typical of the handiwork of the PWD. Bel Retiro acquired a stone wing in 1890, and the northern end of the building, which had been neglected or damaged during the Japanese Occupation, was reconstructed in 1949.

Many of the mainland hill-station bungalows were erected by the PWD, whose other tasks included building and repairing roads. Apparently, most house construction was in the hands of the Chinese, who were assisted, at least in the early years, by Tamil and Javanese coolies, according to Robson's *People in a Native State*. With the exception of The Cottage, which was built of stone and rubble quarried on the spot, the Maxwell's Hill bungalows were timber structures with corrugated iron roofs, whereas the early bungalows at Fraser's Hill were of solid granite with red-tiled roofs.

The typical bungalow on Maxwell's Hill was similar in plan to that of the tea kiosk on Penang Hill. It comprised a front porch and a veranda enclosed with glass-panelled doors, a main central room open from front to back that served as a sitting/dining-room, bedrooms with attached bathrooms along either side of the main room, and a toilet and storage space at the rear, where there were steps down to a covered passage that led to the kitchen and the servants' quarters. No doubt because flat land was scarce at Maxwell's Hill, the typical compound was relatively small; consequently, bungalows and their associated outbuildings were close together.

Rest-houses invariably were bungalows, and each of the hill stations had at least one. They functioned as inns or small hotels and were primarily, though not exclusively, intended to serve the needs of travelling government officers. Overnight visitors sometimes brought their own servants. Furniture, crockery, glass, and linen were supplied by the government, as were the stables, but a visitor's horse had to be attended to by his own syce. In addition to a caretaker, most rest-houses had a cook, a water-carrier, and a 'boy'. A standard feature of the rest-house (and of other dwellings occupied by Europeans) was a bathroom equipped with a huge 'Shanghai jar' (a ceramic receptacle) and a wooden or tin scoop or dipper (or *gayong*). It was not uncommon for a newly arrived European to try to get into the jar, which was also used for keeping beer cold. Etiquette required the bather to dip water from the jar and to use it as a cool and deliciously refreshing douche.

The garden not only expressed nostalgia for home but also maintained and reinforced the identity and separateness of the colonial community. The majority of the British in the civil and military services in India 'came from homes where an interest in gardens was a part of civilized life', according to Mildred Archer, and the same was true of Malaya. Visitors to the Peninsula's little belvederes were invariably expansive over the flowers in the gardens but few had anything to say about garden design.

Most of early Penang's senior Company officials were probably selected from the middle class of the finely graded metropolitan society, and among their landscape tastes and preferences was a love of the informal or 'natural' landscape garden and a growing interest in exotic plants. It is clear from the appearance of the grounds surrounding Suffolk House, the most elegant of the early nineteenth-century residences in the lowlands, that ideas associated with the picturesque landscape garden had reached the island by that time. Suffolk, John Crawfurd wrote in his 1828 book, resembled an 'English gentleman's mansion and park, where clove and nutmeg trees ... are substituted for oaks, elms, and ashes. The grounds contain from two to three hundred spotted deer.'

Most of the bungalow gardens on Penang Hill were probably small, modest creations, although Ward praised them for their elegant tastefulness. They were usually constricted by the steeply sloping local topography, and the garden at Bel Retiro comprised a series of sharply descending terraces (see Plate 17). As the hill retreat of the governor, however, Bel Retiro could boast the largest and most elaborate of the hill-station gardens. Wathen mentions that the bungalow was 'surrounded, and almost concealed, by fine trees, and shrubs of the most beautiful kind', and Ward writes that the garden was stocked with many rich and rare exotics, adding that 'the flowers of our native country flourish there luxuriantly'.

The exotics in the Penang Hill gardens included pineapples and sunflowers (see Colour Plate 6), two New World plants with a long history in South-East Asia; roses, strawberries, and other flora from temperate climates that reminded the hill-station clientele of home; and a selection of flora that was probably introduced from places like India and Burma, the hinterlands of Macao and Canton, and the Moluccas—in all of which it is known that British plant hunters were active in the early nineteenth century. Penang was on a major trade route, so other sources of introduced plants cannot be discounted.

The main features of the Penang Hill gardens during the early 1800s were a lawn–like green sward, scattered shrubs, a few flower beds, and here and there some large trees that were probably remnants of the original rain forest (see Colour Plates 5 and 6). The general effect was one of 'contrived naturalness'. By the mid-nineteenth century, some of the gardens had become more elaborate and showy, reflecting metropolitan taste for greater formality.

Very little has been written about the gardens of the mainland hill stations. On the other hand, a good idea of what British gardens in the lowlands were like in the 1920s can be obtained from Kathleen Gough's *A Garden Book for Malaya*. It is reasonable to assume that the hill-station gardens of the inter-war period were generally similar in layout to those of the lowlands, except that they featured a greater emphasis on flowers from temperate climates. As in earlier periods, the ebb and flow of metropolitan taste in gardens was reflected in the Malayan scene. Gough, who had a garden at Kajang in Selangor between 1910 and 1926 and had both practical and professional horticultural training, wrote that in Malaya 'we have exceptional opportunities for planting gardens that can to a great extent remind us of gardens at home.... I have tried to make my garden to resemble and remind me of a home garden as much as is possible within reason.'

Briefly stated, the garden that the British preferred was semi-formal in design and featured well-kept lawns that evoked restfulness and provided a background to flowers and shrubs; flower beds that were square, circular, or oval in shape; trees to sit under and to shade the house from the back premises; well-chosen and well-disposed shrubs; herbaceous borders; and pot plants like cool-looking ferns or decorative flowering plants. Nearest the house was the flower garden proper, together with beds and borders. Pot plants were displayed on verandas, on stands in the open space below houses raised on pillars, and along the drive or path in front of the house (see Plate 1). As might be expected, numerous plant species from cooler climates flourished in the highlands.

At Maxwell's Hill, Katharine Sim found, in the late 1930s, a mass of flowers: 'The neat green terraces and lawns were bordered with roses, dahlias, montbretia, gloriosa, honeysuckle and morning glory.' The geologist J. B. Scrivenor was greatly delighted with the way the gardens at Fraser's Hill showed what could be done with cultivated flowers and turf: 'The lawns round "The Lodge" would rouse the envy of an English gardener. Every garden is bright with blossom-dahlias, chrysanthemums, geraniums, lupins, salvias, antirrhynums [sic], marigolds and daisies, roses, verbena, fuchsia, petunia, Indian pinks, carnations, pansies, zinnias, coreopsis, gladioli, montbresia [sic], balsams, nasturtiums, corncockles, budleighia, heliotrope, phlox; and sweet-smelling purple violets nestle in their beds.' There were, on the other hand, factors that worked against the development and care of the gardens, among them steep slopes, thin soils, abundant pests, lack of local environmental knowledge, and temporary occupation of the hill-station bungalows.

The siting, demarcation, content, and arrangement of the bungalow-compound ensemble embodied and reflected social status, private or governmental control of space and labour, preferred visual experiences, and a desire for privacy and separateness. The garden within the compound was a particulary important means of maintaining self-identity, while well-loved flora from temperate climates evoked nostalgia. How delightful it was to see the 'lustrous hearted rose—English! Ours!', exclaimed a visitor to Fraser's Hill. Together with a network of shaded paths and tracks and a mosaic of open and wooded spaces, the bungalow-compound ensemble provided the setting for the activities and lifestyles of the peripatetic hill-station clientele.

6
Social Life and Leisure

LIKE their counterparts elsewhere in the upland tropics, Malaya's hill stations were primarily resorts or specialized social places that were frequented by Europeans for fun and relaxation, for social intercourse with family and friends, or for the purpose of making new acquaintances. Intended to resemble and to evoke images of places and landscapes at home, they were developed by, and reflected the socio-cultural background of, the European colonial community in Malaya.

Most members of that community were selected or recruited from the middle class of the metropolitan society, whose social and leisure activities included indoor, family-oriented pursuits like parlour games, playing the piano, or listening to the wireless; taking an interest in gardening or lawn games like tennis or croquet; participating in or watching sports like cricket, golf, polo, or horse-racing; passing the time hunting or shooting; frequenting a private club; or going to a pub, a cinema, a library, a museum, or a ballroom. Outside the home, the trend was for leisure to become increasingly commercialized, and this was particularly the case at the specialized resorts that were developed to cater mainly to the demands of the ever more recreation-conscious middle class. It was the metropolitan resorts, as has been noted, that provided the model or point of reference for the hill stations.

Glimpses of early nineteenth-century Penang Hill, its clientele, and their activities are captured in the paintings of Captain Robert Smith and even more vividly in William Daniell's magnificient coloured aquatints after Smith's paintings. The illustrations show that one duty of native servants was to ward off the tropical sun with a wide parasol. The neo-classical clothing of the visitors has some interest. European men wore close-fitting breeches and cutaway jackets, while the women appeared in soft, high-waisted, tubular dresses of comfortable muslin (see Colour Plates 5 and 6).

The women's costumes were cool and airy, whereas the men's were not, because metropolitan fashion, not the climate, dictated what was worn—and increasingly it was *de rigueur* to be fashionable.

Long dresses, crinolines, petticoats, and bonnets were the 'in-thing' during the late Victorian period, and such enveloping abundance tended to restrict women's participation in outdoor activities (see Plate 2). Later attire featured light, washable dresses for the ladies and two-piece suits of comfortable khaki, white drill, or linen for the men, while the custom of dressing in rather formal attire for dinner was gradually abandoned. But some old traditions died hard. It was still advisable, some thought, to wear light woollen underclothes to absorb the body's perspiration, and the sola topi (or topee) was usually worn outdoors. 'There is no defence for the topee,' R. O. Winstedt protested in the 1930s. He mocked it as a 'fossilized horror', adding that women, 'preferring death from sun-stroke to the dishonour of such a covering, have discarded it'. Freed for a while from the constraints of lowland society, most hill-station sojourners relaxed in airy, comfortable clothing. Photographs of the late nineteenth century show government officers relaxing at Penang Hill in light *tutup* (closed) jackets and sarongs.

To those familiar with the British resorts, Malaya's little belvederes offered few facilities for amusement and leisure. Each was essentially a collection of named bungalows. None could boast a mall with European-style shops; none had a race-course or a polo field (although two had 9-hole golf courses); and none had assembly rooms or libraries of any social importance. There was only a handful of clubs, pubs, and hotels. In short, most of the institutions and facilities that characterized even some of the small Indian hill stations were absent or poorly represented.

In spite of these shortcomings, Malaya's hill stations did possess certain attractions, including diverse topography and generally splendid scenery, interesting and abundant flora and fauna, shaded paths and open spaces for walking and riding, facilities for sports or pastimes like golf, tennis, and croquet, pleasant gardens and secluded bungalows with cool verandas, the company of other Europeans, freedom from the constraints of lowland authority, and opportunities to escape from the perceived baleful effects of the tropical climate and the socially restricting presence of non-Europeans. Most forms of social interaction and leisure took place outdoors—in part because the climate was agreeable, in part because there were few indoor facilities—and tended to follow the dictates of fashionable behaviour in the contemporary metropolitan society.

Penang Hill

A trip to Penang Hill invariably included a visit to the waterfall or cascade some 6–7 kilometres north-west of George Town, which was a popular picnic spot and whose rugged grandeur appealed to early nineteenth-century landscape tastes (see Colour Plate 7). In the anonymous 1828 article, 'Letters from the East—Penang', it was pointed out that 'a leaf-built shed, with a bench, had been placed in a convenient situation opposite to this waterfall, and steps are constructed from the bottom of the hill to this spot; an hospitable arrangement, which facilitates the approach of strangers anxious to view this curious and beautiful phenomenon.' Kinloch was not nearly so impressed. The waterfall, he complained in his 1853 book, 'is a very poor affair, and is scarcely worth a visit'. He probably saw the falls during a dry period, which would account for his disappointment with the scene.

John Cameron mentions that there were bathhouses and a hotel near the falls, which were incorporated, in 1884, into the Waterfall (or Botanic) Garden, also a favourite attraction on the way to the hill station (Colour Plate 11). Ambrose Rathborne was one of many visitors who admired the Garden's beautiful flora and well-laid-out paths, adding that the choicer plants were 'sheltered by small light sheds of split bamboo, and amongst the flowers flit swarms of gorgeous butterflies, which congregate together in large clusters on the ground, forming a mosaic of lovely colours'. Having visited the falls and the botanic garden, the sojourner could continue up the winding path to the hill station, with an occasional stop along the way to admire the ever expanding view of the lowlands or to inspect the rich diversity of the rain-forest flora and fauna.

In his 1864 book, Thomson recalls with pleasure a visit to Penang Hill made some years earlier: 'I ascended the winding zigzag path early one morning, accompanied by a ship captain and a purser. We were mounted on smart little Delhi ponies.... On we went, alternately admiring the expanding landscape, and the gigantic forest trees and ferns [Plate 18].... The air perceptibly cools, the mists are refreshing; and, when we arrive at Strawberry Hill, we are equally charmed by the magnificent wide-spreading prospect and the true welcome of our host. Our first luxury is a

18. Woman leaning against a tree fern, Penang Hill, *c.*1870? (From John Thomson, *The Straits of Malacca, Siam and Indo-China*, 1993.)

bath in cold water.... The gong sounds, and the native servants wait at breakfast-table.... The cool gentle zephyrs blow through the verandah—our enjoyment is thorough.' Thomson then retired to a shady seat commanding a splendid view of the Kedah and Perak mountains and plains, of the narrow strait, and of George Town at the foot of the hills.

Typical outdoor activities at the hill station included an early morning pony ride to Western Hill (see Figure 2), where there was ample open space for exercise on foot or on horseback; collecting specimens of the local flora and fauna in the surrounding forests, which, according to the early nineteenth-century surgeon and naturalist George Finlayson, offered 'endless enjoyment to those attracted to natural history'; walking or going on picnics or shooting expeditions; painting and sketching; or simply admiring the scenery from a good vantage point (Colour Plate 12).

Penang Hill acquired a hotel in 1895. Situated a little below and to the north of Strawberry Hill and occupying the former property of a Scotsman, one Captain Kerr, this was the Crag Hotel, a popular honeymoon resort and a focus of social life at the hill station for several decades (Colour Plate 13). The Crag was acquired around 1905 by the celebrated Sarkies brothers from Armenia, who ran it as a branch of their more famous Eastern & Oriental Hotel in George Town (the Sarkies also established Raffles Hotel in Singapore and the Strand Hotel in Rangoon). A comfortable hostelry, it consisted of a 'village of bungalows' (Colour Plate 14) grouped around or near a large, central building that contained sitting- and dining-rooms.

Hale mentions that the Crag had detached bungalows for families and a bachelor's establishment, which Dr J. J. Abraham described in the early twentieth century as being 'a long one-storyed, wooden, verandahed building of sleeping apartments ... so arranged that the wind swept through them from the open balcony behind, which projected over a precipice with a sheer drop of several hundred feet to the jungle-clad ravines below'. Winding, shady paths connected the bungalows, and a rose garden graced the site of the main building, where there were occasional dances and other social gatherings.

61

Both before and for some time after the completion of the funicular railway (see Plate 3), the visitor to the Crag was conveyed there in a sedan chair from Strawberry Hill. Bicycle-taxis were also available for hire on the hill, and in his 1941 book Carveth Wells recalled that 'marvellous drives can be enjoyed through the jungle, with lovely views of the city [George Town] and the distant shore of the Malay Peninsula'.

Sir Laurence Guillemard, Governor of the Straits Settlements from 1919 to 1927, invariably spent Christmas at what he referred to as 'a delectable bungalow named "Bel Retiro"', and his presence must have lent a certain cachet to social life on the hill, if only for a little while. Apparently, Sir Laurence was fond of staying on for the New Year's race meeting in George Town, at which time, according to Horace Bleackley, he entertained a large house party at his residence on the hill.

Maxwell's Hill

Maxwell's Hill served as a place of resort from the outset. One of its most distinguished early visitors was Sir Frederick Weld, Governor of the Straits Settlements, who stayed at The Cottage in 1886, his wife Alice describing it as 'Wilderness Cottage'. When not dealing with correspondence, Sir Frederick spent his spare time reading or working in the garden. He recorded this in his journal: 'My stay here has done me a wonderful amount of good. Most of the time we have been here it has been like English April weather, without the harsh winds. We had fires every evening, and I have had one to go to bed with, not that the cold made it necessary, but because it looked bright and cheery.'

Only simple pleasures were on offer at Maxwell's Hill, among them cool and bracing air, gardens with flowers and fruits from temperate climates, strollable tree-lined paths, montane flora for the collecting, and splendid prospects of the Perak River valley, of Taiping at the foot of the hills with its limpid lake and surrounding public gardens, and of the coastal plain extending to the Strait of Malacca (Colour Plate 15). Here is part of Sim's evocation of a stay at The Cottage shortly before World War II:

'It was as cool as an English summer, the flowers were English

19. Fallen Sumatran rhinoceros, *c*.1935. The rhino's home range extended up
to the elevation of the hill stations. (From the *Illustrated London News*,
1936, courtesy of Antiques of the Orient, Singapore.)

and one had almost an English energy ... wood and metal were
chill to the touch; the water in the Shanghai jar was tinglingly
cold; one's skin felt cool and dry. How delicious to be cold again
for a little while! ... We played tennis on a court below the house
surrounded by blue morning glory. The mist came down in the
afternoons and people retired to their rooms and wood fires
to sleep. After a large homeside tea we played croquet on the
lawns ... or we walked up Gunong Hijau (Green Mountain) ...
[where] I saw the weird cups of the pitcher–plant and was shown
the pugs of the Hill rhinos [Plate 19], which I confess scared me a
little.... The next day we walked the nine miles down, getting
hotter and hotter as we descended into the tropics again and our
spirits sinking accordingly.'

Fraser's Hill

Leisure activities at Fraser's Hill included golf, tennis, walking on
the jungle paths, admiring the scenery (the only exertion this
required, Scrivenor once quipped, was 'getting out of bed and
looking out of the window'), playing billiards or cards at the

63

branch of the Selangor Club (where there was a dance most Saturday nights), or having a drink at the Maxwell Arms, which was run by Sir George Maxwell's former head 'boy'.

Margaret Wilson was one of many pre-war visitors who greatly enjoyed Fraser's Hill. The air, she thought, was like wine, and she admired the bungalows with real chimneys, 'each set in its own little garden, where all the old English flowers, so dear to us, flourished. Roses, lupins, nasturtiums, holly hocks, bloomed freely, and in rich abundance.' She recalls that the 'holiday makers rent a furnished bungalow, complete with well trained servants—Chinese, of course—who are responsible for the house keeping. Thus, the temporary tenants enjoy all the comforts of a well run hotel, with the privacy of a home. Walking, golf and tennis comprise the outdoor recreations. There is also a Club, at which dances are held once a week for those so inclined. But, I suspect the greatest attraction of all, lay in the fact that one was able to sit round the glorious log fire, which the coolness of the evening made very welcome, and home like.'

Ambrose Pratt was another visitor who delighted in Fraser's Hill, where every peak, he exuded, was 'spangled with handsome private bungalows perched dizzily on the edges of precipitous declivities'. His days there 'were sheer enchantment', with golf or tennis in the mornings, walks or drives in the afternoons; and, of course, there was interesting flora to admire: 'English flowering shrubs overrun the cultivated terraces and invade the jungle. Violets, daffodils, geraniums and primroses are to be found in every sheltered nook.'

There was a diminutive 9-hole golf course in a narrow ravine (see Plates 14a–b), and 'someone with a cruel sense of humour', Sim wrote, 'had built a row of small shelters from which people watched the golfers. This proved popular and highly entertaining.' The ever comical Wells was amused by the bushes of sensitive mimosa—a leguminous shrub that folds and droops at the slightest touch—growing along the edges of some of the fairways. 'Around the golf course this plant comes in useful,' he joked, 'because it was difficult to lose the ball. When it goes into the rough, the rough lies down.'

Cameron Highlands

The largest of the three hotels at Cameron Highlands was the Cameron Highlands Hotel, whose terrace (Plate 20) overlooked the 9-hole golf course. Adjoining the golf course was the Smokehouse Inn (Plate 21), built in the form of an Elizabethan mansion, where visitors could enjoy looking at English flowers and eating strawberries with fresh cream. But probably the most popular place to stay in the late 1930s, according to Anthony Hill, was the Green Cow, owned by one Mrs Rattray, who, apparently, was fondly known as 'Mrs Rats'.

Sim spent a 'lazy week' at Cameron Highlands on the eve of the Japanese Occupation of Malaya. This happy time, she later recalled, was spent 'dancing a little, walking a little, watching fat trout bask in sunny tanks at the Hatcheries, admiring beautiful begonias in

20. Terrace of the Cameron Highlands Hotel, *c.*1938. (From *British Malaya*, 1939.)

21. The Smokehouse Inn, Cameron Highlands, *c.*1939. (From *British Malaya*, 1939.)

the potting sheds at the Agricultural Gardens, drinking hot rum at the Smoke House Inn and gazing with envy at the flowers there; roses and dahlias, stocks and pansies, forget-me-nots and poppies, an English summer, spring and autumn rolled into one'.

One other reminiscence will have to suffice. It comes from a contributor to Charles Allen's *Tales from the South China Sea*, who had this to say of Cameron Highlands: 'It was five-and-a-half thousand feet high, which meant that it was still nice and warm during the days but that the air was fresh and you had wood fires in the evening and blankets on the bed, which was a treat. There was a golf course and lovely walks and horses to ride and a dance in the hotel every Saturday night.' What an abiding love the English had for a fire in the hearth!

In and Around the Bungalow

At all four hill stations a variety of social activities and leisure pursuits occurred in the bungalow compounds, where they were associated in particular with the garden, the veranda, and, to a lesser extent, the sitting-room. Gardening was a popular pastime, especially among women, and so too were garden parties and lawn games like tennis and croquet. The garden was intended primarily for leisure, for preferred olfactory and visual experiences, and for maintaining identity with home and separateness from indigenous cultures. The aim, as already suggested, was to create an English-style garden that featured, among other things, well-loved flowers, fruits, and vegetables from temperate climates.

Then there was the veranda, that cool, airy, and raised place where friends were greeted and entertained, where dogs lolled, children played, vendors displayed their wares, books were read, letters written, music performed and listened to, cards played, plants potted and tended, where breakfast and sometimes other meals were eaten, and where residents lounged in long low rattan chairs with fixed or folding leg rests (see Plate 9).

Though generally less comfortable than the cool veranda, the sitting-room was also a place for leisure pursuits like reading, sewing, playing the piano, or simply lounging in a comfortable chair. A fire was often lit whether it was needed or not, and the sight of it invariably evoked nostalgia for home. The sitting-room (and most other rooms) in a government-owned bungalow was likely to be rather sparsely equipped with furniture made and supplied by the PWD, whereas the same room in a private bungalow was likely to display more clearly the middle-class suburban tastes of the metropolitan society (Colour Plate 16).

Labour

The lifesyle of the hill-station clientele was largely sustained and maintained by the dominance–dependence relationship between the small but powerful European élite and the Asian cultural groups that composed the majority of the population. Although Chinese entrepreneurs played a significant role in the economy of the hill stations—for example, as organizers of transport services and suppliers of provisions, and, at Cameron Highlands, as vegetable growers and shopkeepers—land, labour, and capital were mainly controlled by Europeans.

Virtually everything had to be transported to the hill stations from the lowlands—travellers and their accoutrements, fresh food, prepared drinks and medicines, various household goods, ornamental plants, and even vegetable mould for the gardens. Consequently, there was a demand for bearers, porters, and other coolies, most of whom were Malays or Tamils, as well as for haulage and delivery services. The flow of goods, services, and labour was essentially unidirectional, and it was largely parasitic on lowland land and life. Only Cameron Highlands supplied some of its own needs.

Servants were employed not only to do housework (Plate 22) but also to signal social status, and most European families in the lowlands employed at least a 'boy', a cook, a water-carrier (*tukang ayer*), a groom or chauffeur (syce), an Indian or Chinese nurse (ayah or amah) to look after the children, a gardener (*tukang kebun*), and a washerman (dhoby or dhobi). Well-to-do families usually had much larger bevies of servants. In his 1894 book on British Malaya, Dennys advised his readers that persons 'from a distance renting a hill-bungalow [on Penang Hill] have to take their

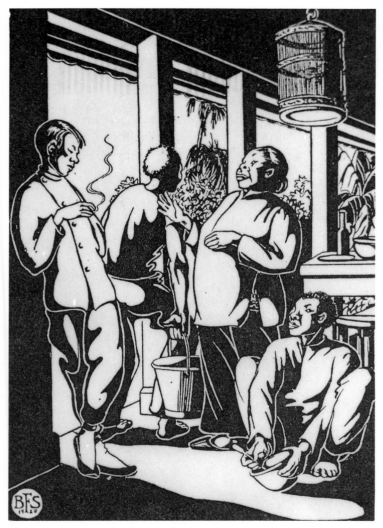

22. Servants on the back veranda: houseboy, water-carrier (*tukang ayer*), Chinese nurse (amah), and cook. (From Ashley Gibson, *The Malay Peninsula and Archipelago*, 1928.)

own staff of servants with them, otherwise they may experience considerable inconvenience on their arrival. Local firms provide the necessary supplies of fresh provisions daily through a coolie, whose charge is 35 cents for each trip up the hill.' It should be kept in mind, however, that the hill stations catered almost entirely to temporary residents, most of whom probably made do with a smaller complement of servants than they were accustomed to in the lowlands. But whether that was the case or not, labour was usually cheap and readily available. The fun and relaxation that Europeans enjoyed at the hill stations was largely made possible by the dualism that characterized colonial society.

Epilogue

MALAYA'S hill stations were small, modestly developed places. Cameron Highlands, it is true, occupied a sprawling site, but its development owed more to the cultivation of tea and vegetables than it did, strictly speaking, to its resort function. Among the factors that conspired to limit both the size and the number of hill stations were the lack of suitable highland sites for such places within easy reach of the main concentrations of Europeans in the lowlands; the generally north–south orientation of the transportation system, which skirted rather than penetrated the uplands; the uniformity of the equatorial climate, which meant that there were no large seasonal migrations to the hills; the fact that it was comparatively easy and inexpensive to travel to a resort in Java or Sumatra; the rather limited amount of private investment in hill-station development; and, of primary importance, the relatively small number of Europeans living in the region at any particular time.

None of the imperial belvederes has grown appreciably since the end of the colonial period in 1957, although numerous proposals for their development have been advanced. In 1979, tiny Maxwell's Hill was renamed Bukit Larut and its old bungalows were stripped of their colonial names, but otherwise it remains largely unchanged. Nor, with the exception of a few new hotels and a variety of rather minor tourist attractions, has there been much development at Fraser's Hill or Penang Hill, while the economy of Cameron Highlands is still mainly based on specialized commercial agriculture. There has, on the other hand, been a change in the composition of the hill-station clientele, most of whom are now domestic holiday-makers and international tourists.

As the Berkeley geographer Robert Reed has pointed out, it has long been an article of faith among scholars that the hill stations of the upland tropics invariably owed their genesis and early development to colonialism. The Peninsula's newest hill station, Genting Highlands, is a major exception to that rule. Situated on the

71

Selangor–Pahang border some 50 kilometres from Kuala Lumpur, to which it is linked by road and helicopter service, Genting Highlands dates from the post-colonial 1960s. Now a sizeable tourist-and-gambling resort with posh hotels (one of which houses Malaysia's only casino), a cable-car system, an 18-hole golf course, and other facilities and amenities, it was founded by two local Asians, not by representatives of Western élites.

The modest development of the older hill stations has been a boon to their surrounding montane forests, which have remained largely intact. But whether this state of affairs will persist is a moot point, because two projects with potentially disastrous ecological consequences have been proposed in recent years. The first was announced in 1988 and involved a scheme to construct a 240-kilometre-long ridge-top road linking Genting Highlands to Fraser's Hill and Cameron Highlands. Environmentalists and nature lovers were justifiably alarmed by this project, which would almost certainly result in massive soil erosion, sedimentation of water courses, widespread forest loss, and elimination of rare or endemic biota. The project has been shelved—permanently, one hopes.

The second project concerns Penang Hill. Announced in 1991, it proposed, among other things, a 200-room hotel on the site of the old Crag Hotel, a condominium development, a cable-car linking the Botanic Garden to the hill station, a shopping and entertainment complex, and a theme park. Opponents of the massive scheme have come together to form an organization called 'Friends of Penang Hill', whose stated goal is to protect the natural and cultural heritage of the hill-station area. The project was in limbo at the time of writing.

Is there scope for hill-station development? The answer is yes, provided it is small-scale, pays attention to the delicate nature of hill-top habitats, and focuses on improving existing hill-station services and facilities. Large-scale projects, on the other hand, are likely to eliminate or greatly alter what would appear to be two of the main attractions of the older hill stations to both local and foreign visitors, namely, their charming tranquillity and their rich and diverse natural settings.

Select Bibliography

Abraham, James Johnston, *The Surgeon's Log, Being Impressions of the Far East*, London, Chapman and Hall, 1911.

Adams, Margaret (comp.), *Penang Illustrated Guide*, Penang, Municipal Council of George Town, 1952.

Aiken, S. Robert, 'Early Penang Hill Station', *Geographical Review*, 77, 1987, pp. 421–39.

Allen, Charles (ed.), *Tales from the South China Sea: Images of the British in South-East Asia in the Twentieth Century*, London, Futura, 1984.

Andaya, Barbara Watson and Andaya, Leonard Y., *A History of Malaysia*, London, Macmillan, 1982.

Archer, Mildred, 'English Gardens in India', *Country Life*, 142, 1967, pp. 1120–3.

Balfour, Andrew, 'Sojourners in the Tropics', *Lancet*, 204, 1923, pp. 1329–34.

Banfield, F. S., *Guide to the Botanic (Waterfall) Gardens Penang*, Penang, Georgetown Printers, 1947.

Banner, Hubert S., 'Hill Station Development in Malaya: Need for More Holiday Resorts', *Field*, 24 May 1929 (supplement), p. 9.

Barr, Pat, *The Memsahibs: In Praise of the Women of Victorian India*, London, Secker and Warburg, 1976.

――――, *Taming the Jungle: The Men Who Made British Malaya*, London, Secker and Warburg, 1977.

Barr, Pat and Desmond, Ray, *Simla: A Hill Station in British India*, New York, Charles Scribner's Sons, 1978.

Bastin, John and Rohatgi, Pauline, *Prints of Southeast Asia in the India Office Library: The East India Company in Malaysia and Indonesia 1786–1824*, London, Her Majesty's Stationery Office, 1979.

Beighton, Thomas, 'Penang: Description of the Island ...', *Chinese Repository*, 3, 1834, pp. 221–30.

'Bengal Civilian' (Charles Walter Kinloch), *De Zieke Reiziger [The Invalid Traveller]; or Rambles in Java and the Straits in 1852*, London, Simpkin, Marshall and Company, 1853; reprinted Singapore, Oxford University Press, 1987.

Bird, Isabella L., *The Golden Chersonese and the Way Thither*, London, John

Murray, 1883; reprinted Kuala Lumpur and Singapore, Oxford University Press, 1967 and 1989.

Bleackley, Horace, *A Tour in Southern Asia (Indo-China, Malaya, Java, Sumatra, and Ceylon, 1925–1926)*, London, John Lane Bodley Head Limited, 1928.

'British Malaya: Travel, Hunting & Investment', *Illustrated London News*, 140 (3809), 1912, pp. 580–1.

Butcher, John G., *The British in Malaya 1880–1941: The Social History of a European Community in Colonial South-East Asia*, Kuala Lumpur, Oxford University Press, 1979.

Cameron, John, *Our Tropical Possessions in Malayan India*, London, Smith, Elder and Co., 1865; reprinted Kuala Lumpur, Oxford University Press, 1965.

Chai Hon-Chan, *The Development of British Malaya 1896–1909*, Kuala Lumpur, Oxford University Press, 1964.

Chronicle of the Development of the Cameron Highlands ..., Kuala Lumpur, Federal Council Paper No. 13, 1932.

Clarkson, James D., *The Cultural Ecology of a Chinese Village: Cameron Highlands, Malaysia*; Department of Geography Research Paper No. 114, Chicago, University of Chicago, 1968.

Cochrane, C. W. H., *Federated Malay States: Annual Report for 1930*, Kuala Lumpur, Federated Malay States Government Printing Office, 1931.

Coote, Philip C., *Peeps at Many Lands: The Malay States*, London, A & C Black, 1923.

Crawfurd, John, *Journal of an Embassy from the Governor-General of India to the Court of Siam and Cochin China*, London, Henry Colburn, 1828; reprinted Kuala Lumpur and Singapore, Oxford University Press, 1967 and 1987.

Cunyngham-Brown, Sjovald, *Crowded Hour*, London, John Murray, 1975.

Davies, Donald, *Old Penang*, Singapore, Donald Moore, 1956.

Dennys, N. B., *A Descriptive Dictionary of British Malaya*, London, 'London and China Telegraph' Office, 1894.

Development of the Cameron Highlands up to the End of 1934 and Information Concerning the Highlands, Kuala Lumpur, Federated Malay States Government Press, 1935.

Edwardes, Michael, *Bound to Exile: The Victorians in India*, New York, Praeger, 1970.

Edwards, Norman, *The Singapore House and Residential Life 1819–1939*, Singapore, Oxford University Press, 1991.

Elliott, Robert, *Views in India, China, and on the Shores of the Red Sea ...*, 2 vols., London, H. Fisher, R. Fisher, and P. Jackson, 1835.

Emerson, Rupert, *Malaysia: A Study in Direct and Indirect Rule*, New York, Macmillan, 1937.

Enriquez, Major C. M., *Malaya: An Account of Its People, Flora and Fauna*, London, Hurst and Blackett, 1927.

Fairlie, John, 'Life in the Malay Peninsula', *Century Magazine*, 45, 1893, pp. 577–87.

Fayrer, Sir Joseph, 'The Hill Stations of India as Health Resorts', *British Medical Journal*, 1, 1900, pp. 1393–7.

Finlayson, George, *The Mission to Siam and Hué the Capital of Cochin China, in the Years 1821–2 ... with a Memoir of the Author, by Sir Thomas Stamford Raffles*, London, John Murray, 1826.

Gibson, Ashley, *The Malay Peninsula and Archipelago*, London and Toronto, J. M. Dent and Sons, 1928.

Gough, Kathleen, *A Garden Book for Malaya*, London, Witherby, 1928.

Guillemard, Sir Laurence, *Trivial Fond Records*, London, Methuen, 1937.

Hale, A., 'Hill Stations and Sanitaria', in Arnold Wright and H. A. Cartwright (eds.), *Twentieth Century Impressions of British Malaya: Its History, People, Commerce, Industries, and Resources*, London, Lloyd's Greater Britain Publishing Company, 1908, pp. 251–2.

Handbook to British Malaya, comp. R. L. German, London, Malay States Information Agency/Malayan Information Agency, 1927 and 1935.

Handbook of the Federated Malay States, comp. H. Conway Belfield, London, Edward Stanford, 1902.

Harrison, Cuthbert Woodville (ed.), *An Illustrated Guide to the Federated Malay States*, London, Malay States Information Agency, 1923; reprinted Singapore, Oxford University Press, 1985.

Hill, Anthony, *Diversion in Malaya: An Incidental Account of Five Years' Residence in the Federated Malay States 1937–1942*, London, Collins, 1948.

Holttum, R. E., *The Waterfall Garden Penang: Illustrated Guide*, Singapore, Government Printer, 1934.

Hoops, A. L., 'The Oldest Straits Settlement: Glimpses of Penang a Century Ago', *Straits Times Annual 1937*, Singapore, Straits Times Press, n.d., pp. 181–91.

Jacob, Gertrude L., *The Raja of Sarawak: An Account of Sir James Brooke, K.C.B., LL.D., Given Chiefly through Letters and Journals*, 2 vols., London, Macmillan, 1876.

Johnson, J., *The Oriental Voyager ...*, London, James Asperne, 1807.

Kaur, Amarjit, *Bridge and Barrier: Transport and Communications in Colonial Malaya 1870–1957*, Singapore, Oxford University Press, 1985.

King, Anthony D., *The Bungalow: The Production of a Global Culture*, London, Routledge and Kegan Paul, 1984.

———, *Colonial Urban Development: Culture, Social Power and Environment*, London, Routledge and Kegan Paul, 1976.

Lennon, Captain Walter Caulfield, 'Journal of a Voyage through the Straits of Malacca and an Expedition to the Molucca Islands ...', *Journal of the Straits Branch of the Royal Asiatic Society*, 7, 1881, pp. 51–74.

'Letters from the East—Penang', *Oriental Herald and Journal of General Literature*, 15, 1828, pp. 281–8.

Lim Chong Keat, *Penang Views 1770–1860*, Singapore, Summer Times Publishing, 1986.

Lovat, Lady Alice, *The Life of Sir Frederick Weld: A Pioneer of Empire*, London, John Murray, 1914.

McMahon, Thomas W. R., *My Reminiscences of a Picnic-Party at Penang, in the Year 1869*, Calcutta, P. S. D'Rozario and Co., 1871.

McNair, J. F. A., *Perak and the Malays: 'Sarong' and 'Kris'*, London, Tinsley Brothers, 1878; reprinted Kuala Lumpur, Oxford University Press, 1972.

Makepeace, Walter, Brooke, Gilbert E., and Braddell, Roland St. J., *One Hundred Years of Singapore*, 2 vols., London, John Murray, 1921; reprinted Singapore, Oxford University Press, 1991.

'Malayan Topics', *Planter*, November 1934, pp. 445–8.

Malaysia and Indo-China: Information for Visitors ..., Singapore, Thomas Cook & Son, 1926.

Maxwell, Sir George, 'The Early Days of Fraser's Hill', *Malaya*, September 1952, pp. 35–7 and October 1952, pp. 23–7.

———, 'Has Gunong Tahan Been Jilted?', *Malaya*, August 1952, pp. 27–9.

———, *Federated Malay States: Annual Report for 1924*, Kuala Lumpur, Federated Malay States Government Printing Office, 1925.

Miller, H. Eric, 'Extracts from the Letters of Col. Nahuijs', *Journal of the Malayan Branch of the Royal Asiatic Society*, 19 (Part II), 1941, pp. 169–209.

Morris, James, 'Hill Stations', in John Gross (ed.), *The Age of Kipling: The Man, His Work, and His World*, New York, Simon and Schuster, 1972, pp. 51–6.

———, *Places*, London, Faber and Faber, 1972.

Morris, Jan with Winchester, Simon, *Stones of Empire: Buildings of the Raj*, Oxford and New York, Oxford University Press, 1983.

Nilsson, Sten, *European Architecture in India 1750–1850*, London, Faber and Faber, 1968.

Panter-Downes, Mollie, *Ooty Preserved: A Victorian Hill Station in India*, New York, Farrar, Straus and Giroux, 1967.

Parkinson, C. N., 'The Homes of Malaya', *Malayan Historical Journal*, 2, 1955, pp. 123–30.

Passengers' Information Bureau, *Illustrated Guide to Penang*, Penang, Criterion Press, 1924.

'The Penang Hills Railway', *Far Eastern Review*, 23, August 1927, p. 362.

Perak Handbook and Civil Service List, 1893, Taiping, Perak Government Printing Office, 1894.

Plumb, J. H., 'The Commercialization of Leisure in Eighteenth-Century England', in N. McKendrick, J. Brewer, and J. H. Plumb (eds.), *The Birth of a Consumer Society: The Commercialization of Eighteenth-Century England*, Bloomington, Indiana University Press, 1982, pp. 265–85.

Pratt, Ambrose, *Magical Malaya*, Melbourne, Robertson and Mullens, 1931.

Rathborne, Ambrose B., *Camping and Tramping in Malaya: Fifteen Years' Pioneering in the Native States of the Malay Peninsula*, London, Swan Sonnenschein and Co., 1898; reprinted Singapore, Oxford University Press, 1984.

Reed, Robert R., 'The Colonial Genesis of Hill Stations: The Genting Exception', *Geographical Review*, 69, 1979, pp. 463–8.

———, 'Remarks on the Colonial Genesis of the Hill Station in Southeast Asia with Particular Reference to the Cities of Buitenzorg (Bogor) and Baguio', *Asian Profile*, 4, 1976, pp. 545–91.

'A Report by the Chief Secretary to Government, Federated Malay States, on a Visit to Cameron's Highlands in March, 1925 ...', Kuala Lumpur, Federal Council Paper No. 13, 1925.

Robson, J. H. M., *People in a Native State*, Singapore, Walter Makepeace, 1894.

———, *Records and Recollections (1889–1934)*, Kuala Lumpur, Kyle, Palmer and Company, 1934.

Sandwith, F. M., 'Hill Stations and Other Health Resorts in the British Tropics', *Journal of Tropical Medicine and Hygiene*, 10, 1907, pp. 361–70.

Scrivenor, J. B., 'Recollections of Cameron's Highlands and Fraser's Hill', *Journal of the Malayan Branch of the Royal Asiatic Society*, 11 (Part 1), 1931, pp. 2–14.

Sim, Katharine, *Malayan Landscape*, Singapore, Donald Moore for Asia Pacific Press, 1969.

Spencer, J. E. and Thomas, W. L., 'The Hill Stations and Summer Resorts of the Orient', *Geographical Review*, 38, 1948, pp. 637–51.

Stratton-Brown, E., 'Looking Back on Selangor in the Nineties', in *Fifty Years of Progress 1904–1954*, Kuala Lumpur, Malay Mail Supplement, 1955.

Thomson, John, *The Straits of Malacca, Siam and China: Travels and Adventures of a Nineteenth-century Photographer*, Singapore, Oxford University Press, 1993.

Thomson, John Turnbull, *Some Glimpses into Life in the Far East*, London, Richardson and Company, 1864; reprinted Singapore, Oxford University Press, 1984.

Trollope, Anthony, *The Tireless Traveler: Twenty Letters to the Liverpool Mercury*, edited with an introduction by B. A. Booth, Berkeley, University of California Press, 1978.

Turnbull, C. M., *The Straits Settlements 1826–67: Indian Presidency to Crown Colony*, London, Athlone Press, 1972.

Voon, P. K. and Khoo, S. H., 'Upland Development and Settlement in Malaysia', *Malaysian Journal of Tropical Geography*, 1, 1980, pp. 43–56.

Walton, John K., *The English Seaside Resort: A Social History 1750–1914*, New York, St. Martin's Press, 1983.

Ward, T. M., 'Contribution to the Medical Topography of Prince of Wales Island, or Pulo Pinang', in *Official Papers on the Medical Statistics and Topography of Malacca and Prince of Wales' Island and on the Prevailing Diseases of the Tenasserim Coast*, Penang, Pinang Government Press, 1830.

Wathen, James, *Journal of a Voyage, in 1811 and 1812, to Madras and China ...*, London, J. Nichols, Son, and Bentley ... and Black, Parry, and Company, 1814.

Wells, Carveth, *North of Singapore*, London, Jarrolds, 1941.

Wilson, Margaret C., *Malaya: The Land of Enchantment*, Amersham, R. Norrie, Mascot Press, 1937.

Winstedt, R. O., *A Herd of Wild Bungalows*, Singapore, Kelly and Walsh, 1934.

Wright, Arnold and Reid, Thomas H., *The Malay Peninsula: A Record of British Progress in the Middle East*, London, Unwin, 1912.

Yvan, Dr, *Six Months among the Malays; and a Year in China*, London, James Blackwood, 1855.

Index

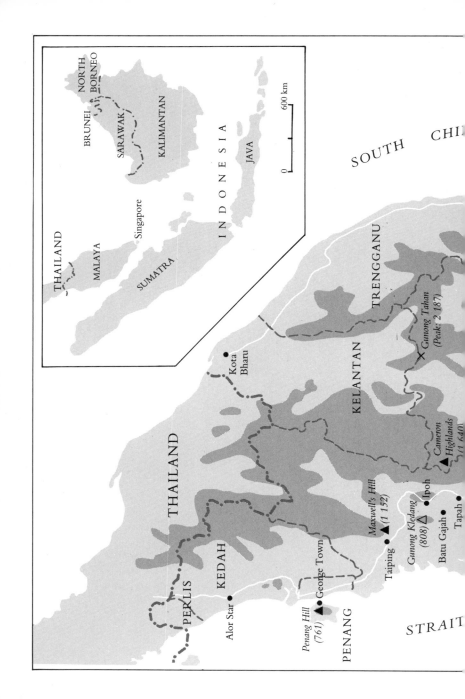

THAILAND

PERLIS

KEDAH

Alor Star ●

Penang Hill
(761) ▲

George Town

PENANG

Taiping ●

Maxwell's Hill
(1 152) ▲

Gunong Kledang
(808) △

Batu Gajah ●

Ipoh ●

Tapah ●

*Cameron
Highlands*
(1 640) ▲

KELANTAN

Kota
Bharu ●

TRENGGANU

✕ *Gunong Tahan*
(Peak: 2 187)

SOUTH CHI[...]

STRAIT[...]

BRUNEI

NORTH
BORNEO

SARAWAK

KALIMANTAN

THAILAND

MALAYA

Singapore

SUMATRA

INDONESIA

JAVA

0   600 km